THE ATHEIST VIEWPOINT

THE ATHEIST VIEWPOINT

Advisory Editor:
Madalyn Murray O'Hair

THE

ORIGIN AND IDEALS

OF THE

MODERN SCHOOL

BY

Francisco Ferrer [y Guardia]

ARNO PRESS & THE NEW YORK TIMES
New York / 1972

Reprint Edition 1972 by Arno Press Inc.

LC# 73-161328
ISBN 0-405-03809-7

The Atheist Viewpoint
ISBN for complete set: 0-405-03620-5
See last pages of this volume for titles.

Manufactured in the United States of America

THE ORIGIN AND IDEALS OF
THE MODERN SCHOOL

THE

ORIGIN AND IDEALS

OF THE

MODERN SCHOOL

BY

FRANCISCO FERRER

TRANSLATED BY JOSEPH McCABE

[ISSUED FOR THE RATIONALIST PRESS ASSOCIATION, LIMITED]

LONDON :
WATTS & CO.,
17 JOHNSON'S COURT, FLEET STREET, E.C.
1913

CONTENTS

INTRODUCTION

————

ON October 12, 1909, Francisco Ferrer y Guardia
was shot in the trenches of the Montjuich Fortress at
Barcelona. A Military Council had found him guilty
of being "head of the insurrection" which had, a few
months before, lit the flame of civil war in the city
and province. The clergy had openly petitioned the
Spanish Premier, when Ferrer was arrested, to look
to the Modern School and its founder for the source
of the revolutionary feeling; and the Premier had,
instead of rebuking them, promised to do so. When
Ferrer was arrested the prosecution spent many weeks
in collecting evidence against him, and granted a free
pardon to several men who *were* implicated in the
riot, for testifying against him. These three or four
men were the only witnesses out of fifty who would
have been heard patiently in a civil court of justice,
and even their testimony would at once have
crumbled under cross-examination. But there was

no cross-examination, and no witnesses were brought before the court. Five weeks were occupied in compiling an enormously lengthy indictment of Ferrer; then twenty-four hours were given to an inexperienced officer, chosen at random, to analyse it and prepare a defence. Evidence sent in Ferrer's favour was confiscated by the police; the witnesses who could have disproved the case against him were kept in custody miles away from Barcelona; and documents which would have tended to show his innocence were refused to the defending officer. And after the mere hearing of the long and hopelessly bewildering indictment (in which the evidence was even falsified), and in spite of the impassioned protest of the defending officer against the brutal injustice of the proceedings, the military judges found Ferrer guilty, and he was shot.

Within a month of the judicial murder of Ferrer I put the whole abominable story before the British public. I showed the deep corruption of Church and politics in Spain, and proved that clergy and politicians had conspired to use the gross and pliable machinery of "military justice" to remove a man whose sole aim was to open the eyes of the Spanish

people. A prolonged and passionate controversy
followed. That controversy has not altered a line of
my book. Mr. William Archer, in a cold and impartial study of the matter, has fully supported my indictment of the prosecution of Ferrer ; and Professor
Simarro, of Madrid University, has, in a voluminous
study of the trial (*El Proceso Ferrer*—two large
volumes), quoted whole chapters of my little work.
When, in 1912, the Supreme Military Council of
Spain was forced to declare that no single act of violence could be directly or indirectly traced to Ferrer
(whereas the chief witness for the prosecution had
sworn that he saw Ferrer leading a troop of rioters),
and ordered the restoration of his property, the case
for his innocence was closed. It remains only for
Spain to wipe the foul stain from its annals by
removing the bones of the martyred teacher from
the trenches of Montjuich, and to declare, with
real Spanish pride, that a grave injustice had been
done.

Meantime, the restoration of Ferrer's property has
enabled his trustees to resume his work. Among his
papers they found a manuscript account, from his
own pen, of the origin and ideals of the Modern

School, and their first act is to give it to the world. In 1906 Ferrer had been arrested on the charge of complicity in the attempt of Morral to assassinate the King. He was kept in jail for a year, and the most scandalous efforts were made, in the court and the country, to secure a judicial murder; but it was a civil (or civilised) trial, and the charge was contemptuously rejected. Going to the Pyrenees in the early summer of 1908 to recuperate, Ferrer determined to write the simple story of his school, and it is this I now offer to English readers.

In this work Ferrer depicts himself more truly and vividly than any friend of his has ever done. For my part, I had never seen Ferrer, and never seen Spain; but I was acquainted with Spanish life and letters, and knew that there had been committed in the twentieth century one of those old-world crimes by which the children of darkness seek to arrest the advance of man. I interpreted Ferrer from his work, his letters, a few journalistic articles he had written—he had never published a book—and the impressions of his friends and pupils. In this book the man portrays himself, and describes his aims with a candour that all will appreciate. The less foolish of his enemies have ceased to assert that he organised or led the riot at Barcelona in 1909. It was, they say, the tendency, the subtle aim, of his work which made him responsible. It may be remembered that the *Saturday Review* and other journals published the most unblushingly mendacious letters, from anonymous correspondents, saying that they had seen posters on the walls of Ferrer's schools inciting children to violence. As the very zealous police did not at the trial even mention Ferrer's schools, or the text-books used in them, these lies need no further exposure. But many persist in thinking, since there is now nothing further to think to the disadvantage of Ferrer, that his schools were really hot-beds of rebellion and were very naturally suppressed.

Here is the full story of the Modern School, told in transparently simple language. Here is the whole man, with all his ideals, aims, and resentments. It shows, as we well knew, and could have proved with overwhelming force at his trial had we been permitted, that he was absolutely opposed to violence ever since, in his youth, he had taken part in an abortive revolution. It tells how he came to distrust violence and those who used it ; how he concluded that the moral and intellectual training of children was to be the sole work of his career; how, when he obtained the funds, he turned completely from politics, and devoted himself to educating children in knowledge of science and in sentiments of peace and brotherhood.

It tells also, with the same transparent plainness, why his noble-minded work incurred such violent enmity. He naively boasts that the education in the Modern School was free from dogmas. It was not, and cannot be in any school, free from dogmas, for dogma means "teaching," and he gave teaching of a very definite character. Mr. Belloc's indictment of his schools is, like Mr. Belloc's indictment of his character and guilt, evidently based on complete ignorance of the facts and a very extensive know-ledge of the recklessly mendacious literature of his opponents. Even Mr. Archer's account of his school is grossly misleading. The Modern School was "avowedly a nursery of rebellious citizens" only in the same sense as is any Socialist Sunday-school in England or Germany ; and the Spanish Government has never claimed, and could not claim, for a moment the right to close it, except in so far as it falsely charged the founder with crime and confiscated his property.

Ferrer's school was thoroughly rationalistic, and this embittered the clergy—for his system was spreading rapidly through Spain—without in the least infringing Spanish law. Further, Ferrer's school explicitly taught children that militarism was a crime, that the unequal distribution of wealth was a thing to be abhorred, that the capitalist system was bad for the workers, and that political government is an evil. He had a perfect right under Spanish law to found a school to teach his ideas; as any man has under English or German law. The prohibited and damnable thing would be even to hint to children that, when they grew up, they might look forward to altering the industrial and political system by violence. This Ferrer not only did not teach, but strenuously opposed. We have overwhelming proof of this at every step of his later career. But he was a child of the workers, and he had a passionate and noble resentment of the ignorance, poverty, and squalor of the lives of so large a proportion of the workers. He was also an Anarchist, in the sense of Tolstoi; he believed that liberty was essential to the development of man, and central government an evil. But, as rigorously as Tolstoi, he relied on persuasion and abhorred violence. I would call attention to Chapter VI of this book, in which he pleads for "the co-education of the rich and poor"; and there were children of middle-class parents, even of university-professors, in his school. Most decidedly he preached no class-hatred or violence. I do not share his academic and innocent Anarchist ideal— which is far nearer to Conservatism than to Socialism —but I share to the full that intense and passionate longing for the uplifting and brightening of the poor, and for the destruction of superstition, which was the supreme ideal of his life and of his work. For that he was shot.

Finally, the reader must strictly bear in mind the Spanish atmosphere of this tragedy. When Ferrer describes "existing schools" he means the schools of Spain, which are, for the most part, a mockery and a shame. When he talks of "ruling powers" he has in mind the politicians of Spain, my indictment of whom, in their own language, has never been questioned. When he talks of "superstition" he means primarily Spanish superstition ; he refers to a priesthood that still makes millions every year by the sale of indulgences. If you remember these things, you will, however you dissent from his teaching in parts, appreciate the burning and unselfish idealism of the man, and understand why some of us see the brand of Cain on the fair brow of Spain for extinguishing that idealism in blood.

J. M.

February, 1913.

Chapter I.

THE BIRTH OF MY IDEALS

The share which I had in the political struggles of the last part of the nineteenth century put my early convictions to a severe test. I was a revolutionary in the cause of justice; I was convinced that liberty, equality, and fraternity were the legitimate fruit to be expected of a republic. Seeing, therefore, no other way to attain this ideal but a political agitation for a change of the form of government, I devoted myself entirely to the republican propaganda.[1]

My relations with D. Manuel Ruiz Zorrilla, who was one of the leading figures in the revolutionary movement, brought me into contact with a number of the Spanish revolutionaries and some prominent French agitators, and my intercourse with them led to a sharp disillusion. I detected in many of them an egoism which they sought hypocritically to conceal, while the ideals of others, who were more sincere, seemed to me inadequate. In none of them did I perceive a design to bring about a radical improve-

[1] This was in the early eighties, when Ferrer, then in his early twenties, was secretary to the republican leader Ruiz Zorrilla. To this phase of his career, which he rapidly outgrew, belongs the revolutionary document which was malignantly and dishonestly used against him twenty-five years afterwards.—J. M.

ment—a reform which should go to the roots of dis-order and afford some security of a perfect social regeneration.

The experience I acquired during my fifteen years' residence at Paris, in which I witnessed the crises of Boulangism, Dreyfusism, and Nationalism, and the menace they offered to the Republic, convinced me that the problem of popular education was not solved ; and, if it were not solved in France, there was little hope of Spanish republicanism settling it, especially as the party had always betrayed a lamentable inap-preciation of the need of a system of general educa-tion.

Consider what the condition of the present genera-tion would be if the Spanish republican party had, after the banishment of Ruiz Zorrilla [1885], devoted itself to the establishment of Rationalist schools in connection with each committee, each group of Free-thinkers, or each Masonic lodge ; if, instead of the presidents, secretaries, and members of the committees thinking only of the office they were to hold in the future republic, they had entered upon a vigorous campaign for the instruction of the people. In the thirty years that have elapsed considerable progress would have been made in founding day-schools for children and night-schools for adults.

Would the general public, educated in this way, be content to send members to Parliament who would accept an Associations Law presented by the monarchists ? Would the people confine itself to holding meetings to demand a reduction of the price of bread, instead of resenting the privations imposed on the worker by the superfluous luxuries of the wealthy? Would they waste their time in futile indignation meetings, instead of organising their forces for the removal of all unjust privileges?

My position as professor of Spanish at the Philotechnic Association and in the Grand Orient of France brought me into touch with people of every class, both in regard to character and social position; and, when I considered them from the point of view of their possible influence on the race, I found that they were all bent upon making the best they could of life in a purely individualist sense. Some studied Spanish with a view to advancing in their profession, others in order to master Spanish literature and promote their careers, and others for the purpose of obtaining further pleasure by travelling in countries where Spanish was spoken.

No one felt the absurdity of the contradictions between belief and knowledge; hardly one cared to give a just and rational form to human society, in order that all the members of each generation might have a proportionate share in the advantages created by earlier generations. Progress was conceived as a kind of fatalism, independent of the knowledge and the goodwill of men, subject to vacillations and accidents in which the conscience and energy of man had no part. The individual, reared in a family circle, with its inveterate atavism and its traditional illusions maintained by ignorant mothers, and in the school with something worse than error—the sacramental untruth imposed by men who spoke in the name of a divine revelation—was deformed and degenerate at his entrance into society; and, if there is any logical relation between cause and effect, nothing could be expected of him but irrational and pernicious results.

I spoke constantly to those whom I met with a view to proselytism, seeking to ascertain the use of each of them for the purpose of my ideal, and soon realised that nothing was to be expected of the politicians who surrounded Ruiz Zorrilla; they were, in my opinion, with a few honourable exceptions, impenitent adventurers. This gave rise to a certain expression which the judicial authorities sought to use to my disadvantage in circumstances of great gravity and peril. Zorrilla, a man of lofty views and not sufficiently on his guard against human malice, used to call me an " anarchist " when he heard me put forward a logical solution of a problem; at all times he regarded me as a deep radical, opposed to the opportunist views and the showy radicalism of the Spanish revolutionaries who surrounded and even exploited him, as well as the French republicans, who held a policy of middle-class government and avoided what might benefit the disinherited proletariate, on the pretext of distrusting utopias.

In a word, during the early years of the restoration there were men conspiring with Ruiz Zorrilla who have since declared themselves convinced monarchists and conservatives; and that worthy man, who protested earnestly against the *coup d'État* of January 3, 1874, confided in his false friends, with the result, not uncommon in the political world, that most of them abandoned the republican party for the sake of some office. In the end he could count only on the support of those who were too honourable to sell themselves, though they lacked the logic to develop his ideas and the energy to carry out his work.

In consequence of this I restricted myself to my pupils, and selected for my purposes those whom I thought more appropriate and better disposed. Having now a clear idea of the aim which I proposed to myself and a certain prestige from my position as teacher and my expansive character, I discussed various subjects with my pupils when the lessons were over ; sometimes we spoke of Spanish customs, sometimes of politics, religion, art, or philosophy. I sought always to correct the exaggerations of their judgments, and to show clearly how mischievous it is — to subordinate one's own judgment to the dogma of a — sect, school, or party, as is so frequently done. In — this way I succeeded in bringing about a certain agreement among men who differed in their creeds and views, and induced them to master the beliefs which they had hitherto held unquestioningly by faith, obedience, or sheer indolence. My friends and pupils found themselves happy in thus abandoning some ancient error and opening their minds to truths which uplifted and ennobled them.

A rigorous logic, applied with discretion, removed fanatical bitterness, established intellectual harmony, and gave, to some extent at least, a progressive disposition to their wills. Freethinkers who opposed the Church and rejected the legends of *Genesis*, the imperfect morality of the gospels, and the ecclesiastical ceremonies ; more or less opportunist republicans or radicals who were content with the futile equality conferred by the title of citizen, without in the least affecting class distinctions ; philosophers who fancied they had discovered the first cause of things in their metaphysical labyrinths and established truth in their empty phrases—all were enabled to see the errors of others as well as their own, and they leaned more and more to the side of common sense.

When the further course of my life separated me from these friends and brought on me an unmerited imprisonment, I received many expressions of confidence and friendship from them. From all of them I anticipate useful work in the cause of progress, and I congratulate myself that I had some share in the direction of their thoughts and endeavours.

Chapter II.

MLLE. MEUNIER

AMONG my pupils was a certain Mlle. Meunier, a wealthy old lady with no dependents, who was fond of travel, and studied Spanish with the object of visiting my country. She was a convinced Catholic and a very scrupulous observer of the rules of her Church. To her, religion and morality were the same thing, and unbelief—or "impiety," as the faithful say—was an evident sign of vice and crime.

She detested revolutionaries, and she regarded with impulsive and undiscriminating aversion every display of popular ignorance. This was due, not only to her education and social position, but to the circumstance that during the period of the Commune she had been insulted by children in the streets of Paris as she went to church with her mother. Ingenuous and sympathetic, without regard to antecedents, accessories, or consequences, she always expressed her dogmatic convictions without reserve, and I had many opportunities to open her eyes to the inaccuracy of her opinions.

In our many conversations I refrained from taking any definite side ; so that she did not recognise me as a partisan of any particular belief, but as a careful

reasoner with whom it was a pleasure to confer.   She
formed so flattering an opinion of me, and was so
solitary, that she gave me her full confidence and
friendship, and invited me to accompany her on her
travels.   I accepted the offer, and we travelled in
various countries.   My conduct and our constant
conversation compelled her to recognise the error
of thinking that every unbeliever was perverse and
every atheist a hardened criminal, since I, a convinced
atheist, manifested symptoms very different from those
which her religious prejudice had led her to expect.

She thought, however, that my conduct was excep-
tional, and reminded me that the exception proves
the rule.   In the end the persistency and logic of my
arguments forced her to yield to the evidence, and,
when her prejudice was removed, she was convinced
that a rational and scientific education would preserve
children from error, inspire men with a love of good
conduct, and reorganise society in accord with the
demands of justice.   She was deeply impressed by
the reflection that she might have been on a level
with the children who had insulted her if, at their age,
she had been reared in the same conditions as they.
When she had given up her belief in innate ideas, she
was greatly preoccupied with the following problem :
If a child were educated without hearing anything
about religion, what idea of the Deity would it have
on reaching the age of reason ?

After a while, it seemed to me that we were wasting
time if we were not prepared to go on from words to
deeds.   To be in possession of an important privilege

through the imperfect organisation of society and by the accident of birth, to conceive ideas of reform, and to remain inactive or indifferent amid a life of pleasure, seemed to me to incur a responsibility similar to that of a man who refused to lend a hand to a person whom he could save from danger. One day, therefore, I said to Mlle. Meunier :—

"Mlle., we have reached a point at which it is necessary to reconsider our position. The world appeals to us for our assistance, and we cannot honestly refuse it. It seems to me that to expend entirely on comforts and pleasures resources which form part of the general patrimony, and which would suffice to establish a useful institution, is to commit a fraud; and that would be sanctioned neither by a believer nor an unbeliever. I must warn you, therefore, that you must not count on my company in your further travels. I owe myself to my ideas and to humanity, and I think that you ought to have the same feeling now that you have exchanged your former faith for rational principles."

She was surprised, but recognised the justice of my decision, and, without other stimulus than her own good nature and fine feeling, she gave me the funds for the establishment of an institute of rational education. The Modern School, which already existed in my mind, was thus ensured of realisation by this generous act.

All the malicious statements that have been made in regard to this matter—for instance, that I had to submit to a judicial interrogation—are sheer calumnies.

It has been said that I used a power of suggestion over Mlle. Meunier for my own purposes. This statement, which is as offensive to me as it is insulting to the memory of that worthy and excellent lady, is absolutely false. I do not need to justify myself; I leave my vindication to my acts, my life, and the impartial judgment of my contemporaries. But Mlle. Meunier is entitled to the respect of all men of right feeling, of all those who have been delivered from the despotism of sect and dogma, who have broken all connection with error, who no longer submit the light of reason to the darkness of faith nor the dignity of freedom to the yoke of obedience.

She believed with honest faith. She had been taught that between the Creator and the creature there is a hierarchy of intermediaries whom one must obey, and that one must bow to a series of mysteries contained in the dogmas imposed by a divinely instituted Church. In that belief she remained perfectly tranquil. The remarks I made and advice I offered her were not spontaneous commentaries on her belief, but natural replies to her efforts to convert me; and, from her want of logic, her feeble reasoning broke down under the strength of my arguments, instead of her persuading me to put faith before reason. She could not regard me as a tempting spirit, since it was always she who attacked my convictions; and she was in the end vanquished by the struggle of her faith and her own reason, which was aroused by her indiscretion in assailing the faith of one who opposed her beliefs.

She now ingenuously sought to exonerate the Communist boys as poor and uneducated wretches, the offspring of crime, disturbers of the social order on account of the injustice which, in face of such a disgrace, permits others, equal disturbers of the social order, to live unproductive lives, enjoy great wealth, exploit ignorance and misery, and trust that they will continue throughout eternity to enjoy their pleasures on account of their compliance with the rites of the Church and their works of charity. The idea of a reward of easy virtue and punishment of unavoidable sin shocked her conscience and moderated her religious feeling, and, seeking to break the atavistic chain which so much hampers any attempt at reform, she decided to contribute to the founding of a useful work which would educate the young in a natural way and in conditions which would help them to use to the full the treasures of knowledge which humanity has acquired by labour, study, observation, and the methodical arrangement of its general conclusions.

In this way, she thought, with the aid of a supreme intelligence which veils itself in mystery from the mind of man, or by the knowledge which humanity has gained by suffering, contradiction, and doubt, the future will be realised; and she found an inner contentment and vindication of her conscience in the idea of contributing, by the bestowal of her property, to a work of transcendent importance.

Chapter III.

I ACCEPT THE RESPONSIBILITY

Once I was in possession of the means of attaining my object, I determined to put my hand to the task without delay.[1] It was now time to give a precise shape to the vague aspiration that had long haunted my imagination; and to that end, conscious of my imperfect knowledge of the art of pædagogy, I sought the counsel of others. I had not a great confidence in the official pædagogists, as they seemed to me to be largely hampered by prejudices in regard to their subject or other matters, and I looked out for some competent person whose views and conduct would accord with my ideals. With his assistance I would formulate the programme of the Modern School which I had already conceived. In my opinion it was to be, not the perfect type of the future school of a rational state of society, but a precursor of it, the best possible adaptation of our means; that is to say, an emphatic rejection of the ancient type of school which still survives, and a careful experiment in the direction of imbuing the children of the future with the substantial truths of science.

[1] Mlle. Meunier died, leaving about £30,000 unconditionally to Ferrer, before he returned to Spain in 1900.—J. M.

I was convinced that the child comes into the world without innate ideas, and that during the course of his life he gathers the ideas of those nearest to him, modifying them according to his own observation and reading. If this is so, it is clear that the child should receive positive and truthful ideas of all things, and be taught that, to avoid error, it is essential to admit nothing on faith, but only after experience or rational demonstration. With such a training the child will become a careful observer, and will be prepared for all kinds of studies.

When I had found a competent person, and while the first lines were being traced of the plan we were to follow, the necessary steps were taken in Barcelona for the founding of the establishment; the building was chosen and prepared, and the furniture, staff, advertisements, prospectuses, leaflets, etc., were secured. In less than a year all was ready, though I was put to great loss through the betrayal of my confidence by a certain person. It was clear that we should at once have to contend with many difficulties, not only on the part of those who were hostile to rational education, but partly on account of a certain class of theorists, who urged on me, as the outcome of their knowledge and experience, advice which I could only regard as the fruit of their prejudices. One man, for instance, who was afflicted with a zeal for local patriotism, insisted that the lessons should be given in Catalan [the dialect of the province of Barcelona], and would thus confine humanity and the world within the narrow limits of the region between the

Ebro and the Pyrenees. I would not, I told the enthusiast, even adopt Spanish as the language of the school if a universal language had already advanced sufficiently to be of practical use. I would a hundred times rather use Esperanto than Catalan.

The incident confirmed me in my resolution not to submit the settlement of my plan to the authority of distinguished men who, with all their repute, do not take a single voluntary step in the direction of reform. I felt the burden of the responsibility I had accepted, and I endeavoured to discharge it as my conscience directed. Resenting the marked social inequalities of the existing order as I did, I could not be content to deplore their effects; I must attack them in their causes, and appeal to the principle of justice—to that ideal equality which inspires all sound revolutionary feeling.

If matter is one, uncreated, and eternal—if we live on a relatively small body in space, a mere speck in comparison with the innumerable globes about us, as is taught in the universities, and may be learned by the privileged few who share the monopoly of science—we have no right to teach, and no excuse for teaching, in the primary schools to which the people go when they have the opportunity, that God made the world out of nothing in six days, and all the other absurdities of the ancient legends. Truth is universal, and we owe it to everybody. To put a price on it, to make it the monopoly of a privileged few, to detain the lowly in systematic ignorance, and —what is worse—impose on them a dogmatic and official doctrine in contradiction with the teaching of science, in order that they may accept with docility their low and deplorable condition, is to me an intolerable indignity. For my part, I consider that the most effective protest and the most promising form of revolutionary action consist in giving the oppressed, the disinherited, and all who are conscious of a demand for justice, as much truth as they can receive, trusting that it will direct their energies in the great work of the regeneration of society.

Hence the terms of the first announcement of the Modern School that was issued to the public. It ran as follows :—

PROGRAMME.

The mission of the Modern School is to secure that the boys and girls who are entrusted to it shall become well-instructed, truthful, just, and free from all prejudice.

To that end the rational method of the natural sciences will be substituted for the old dogmatic teaching. It will stimulate, develop, and direct the natural ability of each pupil, so that he or she will not only become a useful member of society, with his individual value fully developed, but will contribute, as a necessary consequence, to the uplifting of the whole community.

It will instruct the young in sound social duties, in conformity with the just principle that " there are no duties without rights, and no rights without duties."

In view of the good results that have been obtained abroad by mixed education, and especially in order to realise the great aim of the Modern School—the formation of an entirely fraternal body of men and women, without distinction of sex or class—children of both sexes, from the age of five upward, will be received.

For the further development of its work, the Modern School will be opened on Sunday mornings, when there will be classes on the sufferings of mankind throughout the course of history, and on the men and women who have distinguished themselves in science, art, or the fight for progress. The parents of the children may attend these classes.

In the hope that the intellectual work of the Modern School will be fruitful, we have, besides securing hygienic conditions in the institution and its dependencies, arranged to have a medical inspection of children at their entrance into the school. The result of this will be communicated to the parents if it is deemed necessary ; and others will be held periodically, in order to prevent the spread of contagious diseases during the school hours.

During the week which preceded the opening of the Modern School I invited the representatives of the press to visit the institution and make it known, and some of the journals inserted appreciative notices of the work. It may be of historical interest to quote a few paragraphs from *El Diluvio* :—

The future is budding in the school. To build on any other foundation is to build on sand. Unhappily, the school may serve either the purposes of tyranny or the cause of liberty, and may thus serve either barbarism or civilisation.

We are therefore pleased to see certain patriots and humanitarians, who grasp the transcendent importance of this social function, which our Government systematically overlooks, hasten to meet this pressing need by founding a Modern School ; a school which will not seek to promote the interests of sect and to move in the old ruts, as has been done hitherto, but will create an intellectual environment in which the new generation will absorb the ideas and the impulses which the stream of progress unceasingly brings.

This end can only be attained by private enterprise. Our existing institutions, tainted with all the vices of the past and weakened by all the trivialities of the present, cannot discharge this useful function. It is reserved for men of noble mind and unselfish feeling to open up the new path by which succeeding generations will rise to higher destinies.

This has been done, or will be done, by the founders of the modest Modern School which we have visited at the courteous invitation of its directors and those who are interested in its development. This school is not a commercial enterprise, like most scholastic institutions, but a pædagogical experiment, of which only one other specimen exists in Spain (the Free Institution of Education at Madrid).

Sr. Salas Antón brilliantly expounded the programme of the school to the small audience of journalists and others who attended the modest opening-festival, and descanted on the design of educating children in the *whole* truth and *nothing but* the truth, or what is proved to be such. His chief theme was that the founders do not propose to add one more to the number of what are known as " Lay Schools," with their impassioned dogmatism, but a serene observatory, open to the four winds of heaven, with no cloud darkening the horizon and interposing between the light and the mind of man.

Chapter IV.

THE EARLY PROGRAMME

THE time had come to think of the inauguration of the Modern School. Some time previously I had invited a number of gentlemen of great distinction and of progressive sentiments to assist me with their advice and form a kind of Committee of Consultation. My intercourse with them at Barcelona was of great value to me, and many of them remained in permanent relation with me, for which I may express my gratitude. They were of opinion that the Modern School should be opened with some display—invitation-cards, a circular to the press, a large hall, music, and oratorical addresses by distinguished Liberal politicians. It would have been easy to do this, and we would have attracted an audience of hundreds of people who would have applauded with that momentary enthusiasm which characterises our public functions. But I was not seduced by the idea. As a Positivist and an idealist I was convinced that a simple modesty best befitted the inauguration of a work of reform. Any other method seemed to me disingenuous, a concession to enervating conventions and to the very evil which I was setting out to reform. The proposal of the Committee was, therefore, repugnant to my conscience and my sentiments, and I was, in that and all other things relating to the Modern School, the executive power.

In the first number of the *Bulletin of the Modern School*, issued on October 30, 1901, I gave a general exposition of the fundamental principles of the School, which I may repeat here :—

Those imaginary products of the mind, *a priori* ideas, and all the absurd and fantastical fictions hitherto regarded as truth and imposed as directive principles of human conduct, have for some time past incurred the condemnation of reason and the resentment of conscience. The sun no longer merely touches the tips of the mountains ; it floods the valleys, and we enjoy the light of noon. Science is no longer the patrimony of a small group of privileged individuals ; its beneficent rays more or less consciously penetrate every rank of society. On all sides traditional errors are being dispelled by it ; by the confident procedure of experience and observation it enables us to attain accurate knowledge and criteria in regard to natural objects and the laws which govern them. With indisputable authority it bids men lay aside for ever their exclusivisms and privileges, and it offers itself as the controlling principle of human life, seeking to imbue all with a common sentiment of humanity.

Relying on modest resources, but with a robust and rational faith and a spirit that will not easily be intimidated, whatever obstacles arise in our path, we have founded the Modern School. Its aim is to convey, without concession to traditional methods, an education based on the natural sciences. This new method, though the only sound and positive method, has spread throughout the civilised world, and has innumerable supporters of intellectual distinction and lofty principles.

We are aware how many enemies there are about us. We are conscious of the innumerable prejudices which oppress the social conscience of our country. This is the outcome of a medieval, subjective, dogmatic education, which makes ridiculous pretensions to the possession of an infallible criterion. We are further aware that, in virtue of the law of heredity, strengthened by the influences of the environment, the tendencies which are connatural and spontaneous in the young child are still more pronounced in adolescence. The struggle will be severe, the work difficult; but with a constant and unwavering will, the sole providence of the moral world, we are confident that we will win the victory to which we aspire. We will develop living brains, capable of reacting on our instruction. We will take care that the minds of our pupils will sustain, when they leave the control of their teachers, a stern hostility to prejudice; that they will be solid minds, capable of forming their own rational convictions on every subject.

This does not mean that we will leave the child, at the very outset of its education, to form its own ideas. The Socratic procedure is wrong, if it is taken too literally. The very constitution of the mind, at the commencement of its development, demands that at this stage the child shall be receptive. The teacher must implant the germs of ideas. These will, when age and strength invigorate the brain, bring forth corresponding flowers and fruit, in accordance with the degree of initiative and the characteristic features of the pupil's mind.

On the other hand, we may say that we regard as absurd the widespread notion that an education based on natural science stunts the organ of the idealist faculty. We are convinced that the contrary is true. What science does is to correct and direct it, and give it a wholesome sense of reality. The work of man's cerebral energy is to create the *ideal*, with the aid of art and philosophy. But in order that the ideal shall not degenerate into fables, or mystic and unsubstantial dreams, and the structure be not built on sand, it is absolutely necessary to give it a secure and unshakable foundation in the exact and positive teaching of the natural sciences.

Moreover, the education of a man does not consist merely in the training of his intelligence, without having regard to the heart and the will. Man is a complete and unified whole, in spite of the variety of his functions. He presents various facets, but is at the bottom a single energy, which sees, loves, and applies a will to the prosecution of what he has conceived or affected. It is a morbid condition, an infringement of the laws of the human organism, to establish an abyss where there ought to be a sane and harmonious continuity. The divorce between thought and will is an unhappy feature of our time. To what fatal consequences it has led ! We need only refer to our political leaders and to the various orders of social life ; they are deeply infected with this pernicious dualism. Many of them are assuredly powerful enough in respect of their mental faculties, and have an abundance of ideas ; but they lack a sound orientation and the fine thoughts which science applies to the life of individuals and of peoples. Their restless egoism and the wish to accommodate their relatives, together with their leaven of traditional sentiments, form an impermeable barrier round their hearts and prevent the infiltration of progressive ideas and the formation of that sap of sentiment which is the impelling and determining power in the conduct of man. Hence the attempt to obstruct progress and put obstacles in the way of new ideas ; hence, as a result of these attempts, the scepticism of multitudes, the death of nations, and the inevitable despair of the oppressed.

We regard it as one of the first principles of our pædagogical mission that there is no such duality of character in any individual—one which sees and appreciates truth and goodness, and one which follows evil. And, since we take natural science as our guide in education, a further consequence will be recognised ; we shall endeavour to secure that the intellectual impressions which science conveys to the pupil shall be converted into the sap of sentiment and shall be intensely loved. When sentiment is strong it penetrates and diffuses itself through the deepest recesses of a man's being, pervading and giving a special colour to his character.

And as a man's conduct must revolve within the circle of his character, it follows that a youth educated in the manner we have indicated will, when he comes to rule himself, recognise science as the one helpful master of his life.

The school was opened on September 8, 1901, with thirty pupils—twelve girls and eighteen boys. These sufficed for the purpose of our experiment, and we had no intention of increasing the number for a time, so that we might keep a more effective watch on the pupils. The enemies of the new school would take the first opportunity to criticise our work in co-educating boys and girls.

The people present at the opening were partly attracted by the notices of our work published in the press, and partly consisted of the parents of the pupils and delegates of various working-class societies who had been invited on account of their assistance to me. I was supported in the chair by the teachers and the Committee of Consultation, two of whom expounded the system and aim of the school. In this quiet fashion we inaugurated a work that was destined to last. We created the Modern, Scientific, and Rational School, the fame of which soon spread in Europe and America. Time may witness a change of its name—the " Modern " School—but the description " scientific and rational " will be more and more fully vindicated.

CHAPTER V.

THE CO-EDUCATION OF THE SEXES

THE most important point in our programme of
rational education, in view of the intellectual condition of the country, and the feature which was
most likely to shock current prejudices and habits,
was the co-education of boys and girls.

The idea was not absolutely new in Spain. As a
result of necessity and of primitive conditions, there
were villages in remote valleys and on the mountains
where some good-natured neighbour, or the priest or
sacristan, used to teach the catechism, and sometimes
elementary letters, to boys and girls in common. In fact,
it is sometimes legally authorised, or at least tolerated,
by the State among small populations which have not
the means to pay both a master and mistress. In
such cases, either a master or mistress gives common
lessons to boys and girls, as I had myself seen in a
village not far from Barcelona. In towns and cities,
however, mixed education was not recognised. One
read sometimes of the occurrence of it in foreign
countries, but no one proposed to adopt it in Spain,
where such a proposal would have been deemed an
innovation of the most utopian character.

Knowing this, I refrained from making any public

propaganda on the subject, and confined myself to private discussion with individuals. We asked every parent who wished to send a boy to the school if there were girls in the family, and it was necessary to explain to each the reasons for co-education. Wherever we did this, the result was satisfactory. If we had announced our intention publicly, it would have raised a storm of prejudice. There would have been a discussion in the press, conventional feeling would have been aroused, and the fear of "what people would say"—that paralysing obstacle to good intentions—would have been stronger than reason. Our project would have proved exceedingly difficult, if not impossible. Whereas, proceeding as we did, we were able to open with a sufficient number of boys and girls, and the number steadily increased, as the *Bulletin* of the school shows.

In my own mind, co-education was of vital importance. It was not merely an indispensable condition of realising what I regard as the ideal result of rational education ; it was the ideal itself, initiating its life in the Modern School, developing progressively without any form of exclusion, inspiring a confidence of attaining our end. Natural science, philosophy, and history unite in teaching, in face of all prejudice to the contrary, that man and woman are two complementary aspects of human nature, and the failure to recognise this essential and important truth has had the most disastrous consequences.

In the second number of the *Bulletin*, therefore, I published a careful vindication of my ideas :—

Mixed education (I said) is spreading among civilised nations. In many places it has already had excellent results. The principle of this new scheme of education is that children of both sexes shall receive the same lessons ; that their minds shall be developed, their hearts purified, and their wills strengthened in precisely the same manner ; that the sexes shall be in touch with each other from infancy, so that woman shall be, not in name only, but in reality and truth, the companion of man.

A venerable institution which dominates the thoughts of our people declares, at one of the most solemn moments of life, when, with ceremonious pomp, man and woman are united in matrimony, that woman is the companion of man. These are hollow words, void of sense, without vital and rational significance in life, since what we witness in the Christian Church, in Catholicism particularly, is the exact opposite of this idea. Not long ago a Christian woman of fine feeling and great sincerity complained bitterly of the moral debasement which is put upon her sex in the bosom of the Church : " It would be impious audacity for a woman to aspire in the Church even to the position of the lowest sacristan."

A man must suffer from ophthalmia of the mind not to see that, under the inspiration of Christianity, the position of woman is no better than it was under the ancient civilisations ; it is, indeed, worse, and has aggravating circumstances. It is a conspicuous fact in our modern Christian society that, as a result and culmination of our patriarchal development, the woman does not belong to herself ; she is neither more nor less than an adjunct of man, subject constantly to his absolute dominion, bound to him— it may be—by chains of gold. Man has made her a perpetual minor. Once this was done, she was bound to experience one of two alternatives : man either oppresses and silences her, or treats her as a child to be coaxed—according to the mood of the master. If at length we note in her some sign of the new spirit, if she begins to assert her will and claim some share of independence, if she is passing, with irritating slowness, from the state of slave to the condition of a respected ward, she owes it to the redeeming spirit of science, which is dominating the customs of races and the designs of our social rulers.

The work of man for the greater happiness of the race has hitherto been defective ; in future it must be a joint action of the sexes ; it is incumbent on both man and woman, according to the point of view of each. It is important to realise that, in face of the purposes of life, man is neither inferior nor (as we affect to think) superior to woman. They have different qualities, and no comparison is possible between diverse things.

As many psychologists and sociologists observe, the human race displays two fundamental aspects. Man typifies the dominion of thought and of the progressive spirit ; woman bears in her moral nature the characteristic note of intense sentiment and of the conservative spirit. But this view of the sexes gives no encouragement whatever to the ideas of reactionaries. If the predominance of the conservative element and of the emotions is ensured in woman by natural law, this does not make her the less fitted to be the companion of man. She is not prevented by the constitution of her nature from reflecting on things of importance, nor is it necessary that she should use her mind in contradiction to the teaching of science and absorb all kinds of superstitions and fables. The possession of a conservative disposition does not imply that one is bound to crystallise in a certain stage of thought, or that one must be obsessed with prejudice in all that relates to reality.

"To conserve" merely means "to retain," to keep what has been given us, or what we have ourselves produced. The author of *The Religion of the Future* says, referring to woman in this respect : "The conservative spirit may be applied to truth as well as to error ; it all depends what it is you conserve. If woman is instructed in philosophical and scientific matters, her conservative power will be to the advantage, not to the disadvantage, of progressive thought."

On the other hand, it is pointed out that woman is emotional. She does not selfishly keep to herself what she receives ; she spreads abroad her beliefs, her ideas, and all the good and evil that form her moral treasures. She insists on sharing them with all those who are, by the mysterious power of emotion, identified with her. With exquisite art, with invariable unconsciousness, her whole moral physiognomy, her whole soul, so to say, impresses itself on the soul of those she loves.

If the first ideas implanted in the mind of the child by the teacher are germs of truth and of positive knowledge ; if the teacher himself is in touch with the scientific spirit of the time, the result will be good

from every point of view.   But if a man be fed in the
first stage of his mental development with fables,
errors, and all that is contrary to the spirit of science,
what can be expected of his future?   When the boy
becomes a man he will be an obstacle to progress.
The human conscience is in infancy of the same
natural texture as the bodily organism; it is tender
and pliant.   It readily accepts what comes to it from
without.   In the course of time this plasticity gives
place to rigidity; it loses its pliancy and becomes
relatively fixed.   From that time the ideas communicated to it by the mother will be encrusted and
identified with the youth's conscience.

The acid of the more rational ideas which the youth
acquires by social intercourse or private study may
in cases relieve the mind of the erroneous ideas
implanted in childhood.   But what is likely to be the
practical outcome of this transformation of the mind
in the sphere of conduct?   We must not forget that
in most cases the emotions associated with the early
ideas remain in the deeper folds of the heart.   Hence
it is that we find in so many men such a flagrant and
lamentable antithesis between the thought and the
deed, the intelligence and the will; and this often
leads to an eclipse of good conduct and a paralysis of
progress.

This primary sediment which we owe to our mothers
is so tenacious and enduring—it passes so intimately
into the very marrow of our being—that even energetic
characters, which have effected a sincere reform of
mind and will, have the mortification of discovering

this Jesuitical element, derived from their mothers, when they turn to make an inventory of their ideas.

Woman must not be restricted to the home. The sphere of her activity must go out far beyond her home; it must extend to the very confines of society. But in order to ensure a helpful result from her activity we must not restrict the amount of knowledge we communicate to her; she must learn, both in regard to quantity and quality, the same things as man. When science enters the mind of woman it will direct her rich vein of emotion, the characteristic element of her nature, the glad harbinger of peace and happiness among men.

It has been said that woman represents *continuity*, and man represents change: man is the individual, woman is the species. Change, however, would be useless, fugitive, and inconstant, with no solid foundation of reality, if the work of woman did not strengthen and consolidate the achievements of man. The individual, as such, is the flower of a day, a thing of ephemeral significance in life. Woman, who represents the species, has the function of retaining within the species the elements which improve its life, and to discharge this function adequately she needs scientific instruction.

Humanity will advance more rapidly and confidently in the path of progress and increase its resources a hundredfold if it combines the ideas acquired by science with the emotional strength of woman. Ribot observes that an idea is merely an idea, an act of intelligence, incapable of producing or doing anything, unless it is accompanied by an emotional state, a motive element.   Hence it is conceived as a scientific truth that, to the advantage of progress, an idea does not long remain in a purely contemplative condition when it appears.   This is obviated by associating the idea with emotion and love, which do not fail to convert it into vital action.

When will all this be accomplished?   When shall we see the marriage of ideas with the impassioned heart of woman?   From that date we shall have a moral matriarchate among civilised nations.   Then, on the one hand, humanity, considered in the home circle, will have the proper teacher to direct the new generations in the sense of the ideal; and, on the other hand, it will have an apostle and enthusiastic propagandist who will impress the value of liberty on the minds of men and the need of co-operation upon the peoples of the world.

Chapter VI.

CO-EDUCATION OF THE SOCIAL CLASSES

There must be a co-education of the different social classes as well as of the two sexes. I might have founded a school giving lessons gratuitously; but a school for poor children only would not be a rational school, since, if they were not taught submission and credulity as in the old type of school, they would have been strongly disposed to rebel, and would instinctively cherish sentiments of hatred.

There is no escape from the dilemma. There is no middle term in the school for the disinherited class alone; you have either a systematic insistence, by means of false teaching, on error and ignorance, or hatred of those who domineer and exploit. It is a delicate point, and needs stating clearly. Rebellion against oppression is merely a question of statics, of equilibrium. Between one man and another who are perfectly equal, as is said in the immortal first clause of the famous Declaration of the French Revolution ("Men are born and remain free and equal in rights"), there can be no social inequality. If there is such inequality, some will tyrannise, the others protest and hate. Rebellion is a levelling tendency, and to that extent natural and rational, however much it may be discredited by justice and its evil companions, law and religion.

I venture to say quite plainly: the oppressed and the exploited have a right to rebel, because they have to reclaim their rights until they enjoy their full share in the common patrimony. The Modern School, however, has to deal with children, whom it prepares by instruction for the state of manhood, and it must not anticipate the cravings and hatreds, the adhesions and rebellions, which may be fitting sentiments in the adult. In other words, it must not seek to gather fruit until it has been produced by cultivation, nor must it attempt to implant a sense of responsibility until it has equipped the conscience with the fundamental conditions of such responsibility. Let it teach the children to be men; when they are men, they may declare themselves rebels against injustice.

It needs very little reflection to see that a school for rich children only cannot be a rational school. From the very nature of things it will tend to insist on the maintenance of privilege and the securing of their advantages. The only sound and enlightened form of school is that which co-educates the poor and the rich, which brings the one class into touch with the other in the innocent equality of childhood, by means of the systematic equality of the rational school.

With this end in view I decided to secure pupils of every social rank and include them in a common class, adopting a system accommodated to the circum-

D

stances of the parents or guardians of the children ;
I would not have a fixed and invariable fee, but a
kind of sliding scale, with free lessons for some and
different charges for others. I later published the
following article on the subject in the *Bulletin*
(May 10, 1905) :—

> Our friend D. R. C. gave a lecture last Sunday at
> the Republican Club on the subject of " Modern
> Pædagogy," explaining to his audience what we mean
> by modern education and what advantages society
> may derive from it. As I think that the subject is
> one of very great interest and most proper to receive
> public attention, I offer the following reflections and
> considerations on it. It seems to me that the
> lecturer was happy in his exposition of the ideal, but
> not in the suggestions he made with a view to realis-
> ing it, nor in bringing forward the schools of France
> and Belgium as models to be imitated.
>
> Señor C., in fact, relies upon the State, upon
> Parliament or municipalities, for the building,
> equipment, and management of scholastic institu-
> tions. This seems to me a great mistake. If
> modern pædagogy means an effort towards the
> realisation of a new and more just form of society ;
> if it means that we propose to instruct the rising
> generation in the causes which have brought about
> and maintain the lack of social equilibrium ; if it
> means that we are anxious to prepare the race for
> better days, freeing it from religious fiction and from
> all idea of submission to an inevitable socio-
> economic inequality ; we cannot entrust it to the
> State nor to other official organisms which neces-
> sarily maintain existing privileges and support the
> laws which at present consecrate the exploitation of

one man by another, the pernicious source of the worst abuses.

Evidence of the truth of this is so abundant that any person can obtain it by visiting the factories and workshops and other centres of paid workers, by inquiring what is the manner of life of those in the higher and those in the lower social rank, by frequenting what are called courts of justice, and by asking the prisoners in our penal institutions what were the motives for their misconduct. If all this does not suffice to prove that the State favours those who are in possession of wealth and frowns on those who rebel against injustice, it may be useful to notice what has happened in Belgium. Here, according to Señor C., the government is so attentive to education and conducts it so excellently that private schools are impossible. In the official schools, he says, the children of the rich mingle with the children of the poor, and one may at times see the child of wealthy parents arm in arm with a poor and lowly companion. It is true, I admit, that children of all classes may attend the Belgian schools ; but the instruction that is given in them is based on the supposed eternal necessity for a division of rich and poor, and on the principle that social harmony consists in the fulfilment of the laws.

It is natural enough that the masters should like to see this kind of education given on every side. It is a means of bringing to reason those who might one day be tempted to rebel. Not long ago, in Brussels and other Belgian towns, the sons of the rich, armed and organised in national troops, shot down the sons of the poor who were claiming universal suffrage. On the other hand, my acquaintance with the quality of Belgian education differs considerably from that of the lecturer. I have before me various issues of a Belgian journal (*L'Exprèss de Liège*) which devotes an article to the subject, entitled "The Destruction of our National System of Education." The facts given are, unfortunately, very similar to the facts about education in Spain, though in this country there has been a great development of education by religious orders, which is, as everybody knows, the systematisation of ignorance. In fine, it is not for nothing that a violently clerical government rules in Belgium.

As to the modern education which is given in French schools, we may say that not a single one of the books used in them serves the purpose of a really secular education. On the very day on which Señor C. was lecturing in Gracia the Parisian journal *L'Action* published an article, with the title "How Secular Morality is Taught," in regard to the book *Recueil de maximes et pensées morales*, and quoted from it certain ridiculously anachronistic ideas which offend the most elementary common sense.

We shall be asked, What are we to do if we cannot rely on the aid of the State, of Parliament, or municipalities? We must appeal to those whose interest it is to bring about a reform ; to the workers, in the first place, then to the cultivated and privileged people who cherish sentiments of justice. They may not be numerous, but there are such. I am personally acquainted with several. The lecturer complained that the civic authorities were so dilatory in granting the reforms that are needed. I feel sure that he would do better not to waste his time on them, but appeal directly to the working class.

The field has been well prepared. Let him visit the various working men's societies, the Republican Fraternities, the Centres of Instruction, the Workers' Athenæums, and all the bodies which are working for reform,[1] and let him give ear to the language of truth, the exhortations to union and courage. Let him observe the attention given to the problem of rational and scientific instruction, a kind of instruction which shows the injustice of privilege and the possibility of reforms. If individuals and societies continue thus to combine their endeavours to secure the emancipation of those who suffer—for it is not the workers only who suffer—Señor C. may rest assured of a positive, sound, and speedy result, while whatever may be obtained of the government will be dilatory, and will tend only to stupefy, to confuse ideas, and to perpetuate the domination of one class over another.

[1] These societies are particularly numerous in Spain, where the government system of education is deplorable, and schools are often established in connection with them.—J. M.

Chapter VII.

SCHOOL HYGIENE

In regard to hygiene we are, in Spain, dominated by the abominable ideas of the Catholic Church. Saint Aloysius and Saint Benedict J. Labré are not the only, or the most characteristic, saints in the list of the supposed citizens of the kingdom of heaven, but they are the most popular with the masters of uncleanliness. With such types of perfection,[1] in an atmosphere of ignorance, cleverly and maliciously sustained by the clergy and the middle-class Liberals, it was to be expected that the children who would come to our school would be wanting in cleanliness; dirt is traditional in their world.

We began a discreet and systematic campaign against it, showing the children how a dirty person or object inspires repugnance, and how cleanliness attracts esteem and sympathy; how one instinctively moves towards the cleanly person and away from the dirty and malodorous ; and how we should be pleased to win the regard of those who see us and ashamed to excite their disgust.

We then explained cleanliness as an aspect of

[1] It is especially commended in the life of Benedict J. Labré and others that they deliberately cultivated filthiness of person. —J. M.

38

beauty, and uncleanliness as a part of ugliness; and we at length entered expressly into the province of hygiene, pointing out that dirt was a cause of disease and a constant possible source of infection and epidemic, while cleanliness was one of the chief conditions of health. We thus soon succeeded in disposing the children in favour of cleanliness, and making them understand the scientific principles of hygiene.

The influence of these lessons spread to their families, as the new demands of the children disturbed traditional habits. One child would ask urgently for its feet to be washed, another would ask to be bathed, another wanted a brush and powder for its teeth, another new clothes or boots, and so on. The poor mothers, burdened with their daily tasks, sometimes crushed by the hardness of the circumstances in which their life was passed, and probably under the influence of religious teaching, endeavoured to stop their petitions; but in the end the new life introduced into the home by the child triumphed, a welcome presage of the regeneration which rational education will one day accomplish.

I entrusted the expounding of the principles of scholastic hygiene to competent men, and Dr. Martínez Vargas and others wrote able and detailed articles on the subject in the *Bulletin*. Other articles were written on the subject of games and play, on the lines of modern pædagogy.[1]

[1] These articles are reproduced in the Spanish edition. As they are not from Ferrer's pen, I omit them.—J. M.

Chapter VIII.

THE TEACHERS

The choice of teachers was another point of great difficulty. The tracing of a programme of rational instruction once accomplished, it remained to choose teachers who were competent to carry it out, and I found that in fact no such persons existed. We were to illustrate once more that a need creates its own organs.

Certainly there were plenty of teachers. Teaching, though not very lucrative, is a profession by which a man can support himself. There is not a universal truth in the popular proverb which says of an unfortunate man: "He is hungrier than a schoolmaster."[1] The truth is that in many parts of Spain the schoolmaster forms part of the local governing clique, with the priest, the doctor, the shopkeeper, and the moneylender (who is often one of the richest men in the place, though he contributes least to its welfare). The master receives a municipal salary, and has a certain influence which may at times secure material advantages. In larger towns the master, if he is not

[1] £20 a year is a not uncommon salary of masters and mistresses in Spain, and many cannot obtain even that.—J. M.

content with his salary, may give lessons in private schools, where, in accord with the provincial institute, he prepares young men for the University. Even if he does not obtain a position of distinction, he lives as well as the generality of his fellow townsmen.

There are, moreover, teachers in what are called "secular schools"—a name imported from France, where it arose because the schooling was formerly exclusively clerical and conducted by religious bodies. This is not the case in Spain; however Christian the teaching is, it is always given by lay masters. However, the Spanish lay teachers, inspired by sentiments of freethought and political radicalism, were rather anti-Catholic and anti-clerical than Rationalist, in the best sense of the word.

Professional teachers have to undergo a special preparation for the task of imparting scientific and rational instruction. This is difficult in all cases, and is sometimes rendered impossible by the difficulties caused by habits of routine. On the other hand, those who had had no pædagogical experience, and offered themselves for the work out of pure enthusiasm for the idea, stood in even greater need of preparatory study. The solution of the problem was very difficult, because there was no other place but the rational school itself for making this preparation.

The excellence of the system saved us. Once the Modern School had been established by private initiative, with a firm determination to be guided by the ideal, the difficulties began to disappear. Every dogmatic imposition was detected and rejected,

every excursion or deviation in the direction of meta-
physics was at once abandoned, and experience
gradually formed a new and salutary pædagogical
science. This was due, not merely to my zeal and
vigilance, but to my earliest teachers, and to some
extent to the naive expressions of the pupils themselves. We may certainly say that if a need creates
an organ, the organ speedily meets the need.

Nevertheless, in order to complete my work, I
established a Rationalist Normal School for the
education of teachers, under the direction of an
experienced master and with the co-operation of
the teachers in the Modern School. In this a
number of young people of both sexes were trained,
and they worked excellently until the despotic
authorities, yielding to our obscure and powerful
enemies, put a stop to our work, and flattered themselves that they had destroyed it for ever.

Chapter IX

THE REFORM OF THE SCHOOL

There are two ways open to those who seek to reform the education of children. They may seek to transform the school by studying the child and proving scientifically that the actual scheme of instruction is defective, and must be modified; or they may found new schools in which principles may be directly applied in the service of that ideal which is formed by all who reject the conventions, the cruelty, the trickery, and the untruth which enter into the bases of modern society.

The first method offers great advantages, and is in harmony with the evolutionary conception which men of science regard as the only effective way of attaining the end. They are right in theory, as we fully admit. It is evident that the progress of psychology and physiology must lead to important changes in educational methods; that the teachers, being now in a better position to understand the child, will make their teaching more in conformity with natural laws. I further grant that this evolution will proceed in the direction of greater liberty, as I am convinced that violence is the method of ignorance, and that the educator who is really worthy of the name will gain everything by spontaneity; he will know the child's needs, and will be able to promote its development by giving it the greatest possible satisfaction.

In point of fact, however, I do not think that those who are working for the regeneration of humanity have much to hope from this side. Rulers have always taken care to control the education of the people; they know better than any that their power is based entirely on the school, and they therefore insist on retaining their monopoly of it. The time has gone by when rulers could oppose the spread of instruction and put limits to the education of the masses. Such a policy was possible formerly because economic life was consistent with general ignorance, and this ignorance facilitated despotism. The circumstances have changed, however. The progress of science and our repeated discoveries have revolutionised the conditions of labour and production. It is no longer possible for the people to remain ignorant; education is absolutely necessary for a nation to maintain itself and make headway against its economic competitors. Recognising this, the rulers have sought to give a more and more complete organisation to the school, not because they look to education to regenerate society, but because they need more competent workers to sustain industrial enterprises and enrich their cities. Even the most reactionary rulers have learned this lesson; they clearly understand that the old policy was dangerous to the economic life of nations, and that it was necessary to adapt popular education to the new conditions.

It would be a serious mistake to think that the ruling classes have not foreseen the danger to themselves of the intellectual development of the people, and have not understood that it was necessary to change their methods. In fact, their methods have been adapted to the new conditions of life ; they have sought to gain control of the ideas which are in course of evolution. They have endeavoured to preserve the beliefs on which social discipline had been grounded, and to give to the results of scientific research and the ideas involved in them a meaning which will not be to the disadvantage of existing institutions ; and it is this that has induced them to assume control of the school. In every country the governing classes, which formerly left the education of the people to the clergy, as these were quite willing to educate in a sense of obedience to authority, have now themselves undertaken the direction of the schools.

The danger to them consists in the stimulation of the human mind by the new spectacle of life and the possible rise of thoughts of emancipation in the depths of their hearts. It would have been folly to struggle against the evolving forces ; the effect would be only to inflame them, and, instead of adhering to earlier methods of government, they would adopt new and more effective methods. It did not require any extraordinary genius to discover the solution. The course of events itself suggested to those who were in power the way in which they were to meet the difficulties which threatened ; they built schools, they sought generously to extend the sphere of education, and if there were at one point a few who resisted this impulse—as certain tendencies favoured one or other of the political parties—all soon understood that it was better to yield, and that the best policy was to find some new way of defending their interests and principles.   There were then sharp struggles for the control of the schools, and these struggles continue to-day in every civilised country ; sometimes the republican middle-class triumphs, sometimes the clergy.   All parties appreciate the importance of the issue, and they shrink from no sacrifice to win the victory.   " The school " is the cry of every party. The public good must be recognised in this zeal. Everybody seeks to raise himself and improve his condition by education.   In former times it might have been said : " Those people want to keep thee in ignorance in order the better to exploit thee : we want to see thee educated and free."   That is no longer possible ; schools of all kinds rise on every side.

In regard to this general change of ideas among the governing classes as to the need of schools, I may state certain reasons for distrusting their intentions and doubting the efficacy of the means of reform which are advocated by certain writers.   As a rule, these reformers care little about the social significance of education ; they are men who eagerly embrace scientific truth, but eliminate all that is foreign to the object of their studies.   They are patiently endeavour-

ing to understand the child, and are eager to know
—though their science is young, it must be remembered—what are the best methods to promote its
intellectual development.

This kind of professional indifference is, in my
opinion, very prejudicial to the cause they seek to
serve. I do not in the least think them insensible of
the realities of the social world, and I know that they
believe that the public welfare will be greatly furthered
by their labours. "Seeking to penetrate the secrets
of the life of man," they reflect, "and unravelling the
normal process of his physical and psychic development, we shall direct education into a channel which
will be favourable to the liberation of energy. We
are not immediately concerned with the reform of the
school, and indeed we are unable to say exactly what
lines it should follow. We will proceed slowly, knowing that, from the very nature of things, the reform of
the school will result from our research. If you ask
us what are our hopes, we will grant that, like you, we
foresee a revolution in the sense of a placing of the
child and humanity under the direction of science ;
yet even in this case we are persuaded that our work
makes for that object, and will be the speediest and
surest means of promoting it."

This reasoning is evidently logical. No one could
deny this, yet there is a considerable degree of fallacy
in it, and we must make this clear. If the ruling
classes have the same ideas as the reformers, if they
are really impelled by a zeal for the continuous re-
organisation of society until poverty is at last elimi-

nated, we might recognise that the power of science is enough to improve the lot of peoples. Instead of this, however, we see clearly that the sole aim of those who strive to attain power is the defence of their own interests, their own advantage, and the satisfaction of their personal desires. For some time now we have ceased to accept the phrases with which they disguise their ambitions. It is true that there are some in whom we may find a certain amount of sincerity, and who imagine at times that they are impelled by a zeal for the good of their fellows. But these become rarer and rarer, and the positivism of the age is very severe in raising doubts as to the real intentions of those who govern us.

And just as they contrived to adapt themselves when the necessity arose, and prevented education from becoming a danger, they also succeeded in organising the school in accord with the new scientific ideas in such a way that nothing should endanger their supremacy. These ideas are difficult to accept, and one needs to keep a sharp look-out for successful methods and see how things are arranged so as to avoid verbal traps. How much has been, and is, expected of education! Most progressive people expect everything of it, and, until recent years, many did not understand that instruction alone leads to illusions. Much of the knowledge actually imparted in schools is useless; and the hope of reformers has been void because the organisation of the school, instead of serving an ideal purpose, has become one of the most powerful instruments of servitude in the hands of the ruling class. The teachers are merely conscious or unconscious organs of their will, and have been trained on their principles. From their tenderest years, and more drastically than anybody, they have endured the discipline of authority. Very few have escaped this despotic domination; they are generally powerless against it, because they are oppressed by the scholastic organisation to such an extent that they have nothing to do but obey. It is unnecessary here to describe that organisation. One word will suffice to characterise it—Violence. The school dominates the children physically, morally, and intellectually, in order to control the development of their faculties in the way desired, and deprives them of contact with nature in order to modify them as required. This is the explanation of the failure; the eagerness of the ruling class to control education and the bankruptcy of the hopes of reformers. "Education" means in practice domination or domestication. I do not imagine that these systems have been put together with the deliberate aim of securing the desired results. That would be a work of genius. But things have happened just as if the actual scheme of education corresponded to some vast and deliberate conception; it could not have been done better. To attain it teachers have inspired themselves solely with the principles of discipline and authority, which always appeal to social organisers; such men have only one clear idea and one will—the children must learn to obey, to believe, and to think according to the prevailing social dogmas. If this were the aim, education could not be other

E

than we find it to-day. There is no question of promoting the spontaneous development of the child's
faculties, or encouraging it to seek freely the satisfaction of its physical, intellectual, and moral needs.
There is question only of imposing ready-made ideas
on it, of preventing it from ever thinking otherwise
than is required for the maintenance of existing social
institutions—of making it, in a word, an individual
rigorously adapted to the social mechanism.

It cannot be expected that this kind of education
will have any influence on the progress of humanity.
I repeat that it is merely an instrument of domination
in the hands of the ruling classes, who have never
sought to uplift the individual, and it is quite useless
to expect any good from the schools of the present
day. What they have done up to the present they
will continue to do in the future. There is no reason
whatever why they should adopt a different system ;
they have resolved to use education for their purposes,
and they will take advantage of every improvement of
it. If only they preserve the spirit of the school and
the authoritative discipline which rules it, every innovation will tend to their advantage. For this they
will keep a constant watch, and take care that their
interests are secured.

I would fix the attention of my readers on this
point : the whole value of education consists in
respect for the physical, intellectual, and moral
faculties of the child. As in science, the only
possible demonstration is demonstration by facts ;
education is not worthy of the name unless it be

stripped of all dogmatism, and unless it leaves to the child the direction of its powers and is content to support them in their manifestations. But nothing is easier than to alter this meaning of education, and nothing more difficult than to respect it. The teacher is always imposing, compelling, and using violence ; the true educator is the man who does not impose his own ideas and will on the child, but appeals to its own energies.

From this we can understand how easily education is conducted, and how light is the task of those who seek to dominate the individual. The best conceivable methods become in their hands so many new and more effective means of despotism. Our ideal is that of science ; we appeal to it in demanding the power to educate the child by fostering its development and procuring a satisfaction of its needs as they manifest themselves.

We are convinced that the education of the future will be entirely spontaneous. It is plain that we cannot wholly realise this, but the evolution of methods in the direction of a broader comprehension of life and the fact that all improvement involves the suppression of violence indicate that we are on solid ground when we look to science for the liberation of the child.

Is this the ideal of those who actually control the scholastic system ? Is this what they propose to bring about ? Are they eager to abandon violence ? Only in the sense that they employ new and more effective methods to attain the same end—that is to say, the formation of individuals who will accept all the conventions, all the prejudices, and all the untruths on which society is based.

We do not hesitate to say that we want men who will continue unceasingly to develop ; men who are capable of constantly destroying and renewing their surroundings and renewing themselves ; men whose intellectual independence is their supreme power, which they will yield to none ; men always disposed for things that are better, eager for the triumph of new ideas, anxious to crowd many lives into the one life they have. Society fears such men ; you cannot expect it to set up a system of education which will produce them.

What, then, is our mission ? What is the policy we must adopt in order to contribute to the reform of the school ?

Let us follow closely the work of the experts who are engaged in the study of the child, and let us endeavour to find a way of applying their principles to the education we seek to establish, aiming at an increasingly complete emancipation of the individual. But how are we to do this ? By putting our hand energetically to the work, by promoting the establishment of new schools in which, as far as possible, there shall rule this spirit of freedom which, we feel, will colour the whole education of the future.

We have already had proof that it leads to excellent results. We can destroy whatever there is in the actual school that savours of violence, all the artificial devices by which the children are estranged from nature and life, the intellectual and moral discipline which has been used to impose ready-made thoughts, all beliefs which deprave and enervate the will. Without fear of injury we may place the child in a proper and natural environment, in which it will find itself in contact with all that it loves, and where vital impressions will be substituted for the wearisome reading of books. If we do no more than this, we shall have done much towards the emancipation of the child.

In such an environment we may freely make use of the data of science and work with profit. It is true that we could not realise all our hopes; that often we shall find ourselves compelled, from lack of knowledge, to use the wrong means. But we shall be sustained by the confident feeling that, without having achieved our entire aim, we shall have done a great deal more than is being done by the actual school. I would rather have the free spontaneity of a child who knows nothing than the verbal knowledge and intellectual deformation of one that has experienced the existing system of education.

What we have sought to do in Barcelona is being done by others in various places. All of us saw that the work was possible. Dedicate yourself to it at once. We do not hope that the studies of children will be suspended that we may regenerate the school. Let us apply what we know, and go on learning and applying. A scheme of rational education is already possible, and in such schools as we advocate the children may develop freely according to their aspirations.   Let us endeavour to improve and extend the work.

Those are our aims.   We know well the difficulties we have to face ; but we have made a beginning in the conviction that we shall be assisted in our task by those who work in their various spheres to deliver men from the dogmas and conventions which secure the prolongation of the present unjust arrangement of society.

Chapter X.

NO REWARD OR PUNISHMENT

RATIONAL education is, above all things, a means of defence against error and ignorance. To ignore truth and accept absurdities is, unhappily, a common feature in our social order; to that we owe the distinction of classes and the persistent antagonism of interests. Having admitted and practised the co-education of boys and girls, of rich and poor—having, that is to say, started from the principle of solidarity and equality—we are not prepared to create a new inequality. Hence in the Modern School there will be no rewards and no punishments; there will be no examinations to puff up some children with the flattering title of "excellent," to give others the vulgar title of "good," and make others unhappy with a consciousness of incapacity and failure.

These features of the existing official and religious schools, which are quite in accord with their reactionary environment and aim, cannot, for the reasons I have given, be admitted into the Modern School. Since we are not educating for a specific purpose, we cannot determine the capacity or incapacity of the child. When we teach a science, or art, or trade, or some subject requiring special conditions, an examination may be useful, and there may be reason to give a diploma or refuse one ; I neither affirm nor deny it. But there is no such specialism in the Modern School. The characteristic note of the school, distinguishing it even from some which pass as progressive models, is that in it the faculties of the children shall develop freely without subjection to any dogmatic patron, not even to what it may consider the body of convictions of the founder and teachers ; every pupil shall go forth from it into social life with the ability to be his own master and guide his own life in all things.

Hence, if we were rationally prevented from giving prizes, we could not impose penalties, and no one would have dreamed of doing so in our school if the idea had not been suggested from without. Sometimes parents came to me with the rank proverb, "Letters go in with blood," on their lips, and begged me to punish their children. Others who were charmed with the precocious talent of their children wanted to see them shine in examinations and exhibit medals. We refused to admit either prizes or punishments, and sent the parents away. If any child were conspicuous for merit, application, laziness, or bad conduct, we pointed out to it the need of accord, or the unhappiness of lack of accord, with its own welfare and that of others, and the teacher might give a lecture on the subject. Nothing more was done, and the parents were gradually reconciled to the system, though they often had to be corrected in their errors and prejudices by their own children.

Nevertheless, the old prejudice was constantly recurring, and I saw that I had to repeat my arguments with the parents of new pupils. I therefore wrote the following article in the *Bulletin* :—

The conventional examinations which we usually find held at the end of a scholastic year, to which our fathers attached so much importance, have had no result at all ; or, if any result, a bad one. These functions and their accompanying solemnities seem to have been instituted for the sole purpose of satisfying the vanity of parents and the selfish interests of many teachers, and in order to put the children to torture before the examination and make them ill afterwards. Each father wants his child to be presented in public as one of the prodigies of the college, and regards him with pride as a learned man in miniature. He does not notice that for a fortnight or so the child suffers exquisite torture. As things are judged by external appearances, it is not thought that there is any real torture, as there is not the least scratch visible on the skin......

The parent's lack of acquaintance with the natural disposition of the child, and the iniquity of putting it in false conditions so that its intellectual powers, especially in the sphere of memory, are artificially stimulated, prevent the parent from seeing that this measure of personal gratification may, as has happened in many cases, lead to illness and to the moral, if not the physical, death of the child.

On the other hand, the majority of teachers, being mere stereotypers of ready - made phrases and mechanical inoculators, rather than *moral fathers* of their pupils, are concerned in these examinations with their own personality and their economic interests. Their object is to let the parents and the others who are present at the public display see that, under their guidance, the child has learned a good deal, that its knowledge is greater in quantity and quality than could have been expected of its tender years and in view of the short time that it has been under the charge of this very skilful teacher.

In addition to this wretched vanity, which is satisfied at the cost of the moral and physical life of the child, the teachers are anxious to elicit compliments from the parents and the rest of the audience, who know nothing of the real state of things, as a kind of advertisement of the prestige of their particular school.

Briefly, we are inexorably opposed to holding public examinations. In our school everything must be done for the advantage of the pupil. Everything that does not conduce to this end must be recognised as opposed to the natural spirit of positive education. Examinations do no good, and they do much harm to the child. Besides the illness of which we have already spoken, the nervous system of the child suffers, and a kind of temporary paralysis is inflicted on its conscience by the immoral features of the examination ; the vanity provoked in those who are placed highest, envy and humiliation, grave obstacles to sound growth, in those who have failed, and in all of them the germs of most of the sentiments which go to the making of egoism.

In a later number of the *Bulletin* I found it necessary to return to the subject :—

We frequently receive letters from Workers'

Educational Societies and Republican Fraternities asking that the teachers shall chastise the children in our schools. We ourselves have been disgusted, during our brief excursions, to find material proofs of the fact which is at the base of this request ; we have seen children on their knees, or in other attitudes of punishment.

These irrational and atavistic practices must disappear. Modern pædagogy entirely discredits them. The teachers who offer their services to the Modern School, or ask our recommendation to teach in similar schools, must refrain from any moral or material punishment, under penalty of being disqualified permanently. Scolding, impatience, and anger ought to disappear with the ancient title of "master." In free schools all should be peace, gladness, and fraternity. We trust that this will suffice to put an end to these practices, which are most improper in people whose sole ideal is the training of a generation fitted to establish a really fraternal, harmonious, and just state of society.

CHAPTER XI.

THE GENERAL PUBLIC AND
THE LIBRARY

In setting out to establish a rational school for the purpose of preparing children for their entry into the free solidarity of humanity, the first problem that confronted us was the selection of books. The whole educational luggage of the ancient system was an incoherent mixture of science and faith, reason and unreason, good and evil, human experience and revelation, truth and error ; in a word, totally unsuited to meet the new needs that arose with the formation of a new school.

If the school has been from remote antiquity equipped not for teaching in the broad sense of communicating to the rising generation the gist of the knowledge of previous generations, but for teaching on the basis of authority and the convenience of the ruling classes, for the purpose of making children humble and submissive, it is clear that none of the books hitherto used would suit us. But the severe logic of this position did not at once convince me. I refused to believe that the French democracy, which worked so zealously for the separation of Church and State, incurred the anger of the clericals, and adopted obligatory secular instruction, would resign itself to a semi-education or a sophisticated education.   I had, however, to yield to the evidence, against my prejudice.   I first read a large number of works in the French code of secular instruction, and found that God was replaced by the State, Christian virtue by civic duty, religion by patriotism, submission to the king, the aristocracy, and the clergy by subservience to the official, the proprietor, and the employer.   Then I consulted an eminent Freethinker who held high office in the Ministry of Public Instruction, and, when I had told him my desire to see the books they used, which I understood to be purged of traditional errors, and explained my design and ideal to him, he told me frankly that they had nothing of the sort ; all their books were, more or less cleverly and insidiously, tainted with untruth, which is the indispensable cement of social inequality.   When I further asked if, seeing that they had replaced the decaying idol of deity by the idol of oligarchic despotism, they had not at least some book dealing with the origin of religion, he said that there was none ; but he knew one which would suit me—Malvert's *Science and Religion*.   In point of fact, this was already translated into Spanish, and was used as a reading-book in the Modern School, with the title *Origin of Christianity*.

In Spanish literature I found several works written by a distinguished author, of some eminence in science, who had produced them rather in the interest of the publishers than with a view to the education of

children. Some of these were at first used in the
Modern School, but, though one could not accuse
them of error, they lacked the inspiration of an ideal
and were poor in method. I communicated with this
author with a view to interesting him in my plans and
inducing him to write books for me, but his publishers
held him to a certain contract and he could not oblige
me.

In brief, the Modern School was opened before a
single work had been chosen for its library, but it was
not long before the first appeared—a brilliant book by
Jean Grave, which has had a considerable influence
on our schools. His work, *The Adventures of Nono*,
is a kind of poem in which a certain phase of the
happier future is ingeniously and dramatically con-
trasted with the sordid realities of the present social
order ; the delights of the land of Autonomy are con-
trasted with the horrors of the kingdom of Argirocracy.
The genius of Grave has raised the work to a height
at which it escapes the strictures of the sceptical and
conservative ; he has depicted the social evils of the
present truthfully and without exaggeration. The reading of the book enchanted the children, and the pro-
fundity of his thought suggested many opportune
comments to the teachers. In their play the children
used to act scenes from Autonomy, and their parents
detected the causes of their hardships in the constitution of the kingdom of Argirocracy.

It was announced in the *Bulletin* and other journals
that prizes were offered for the best manuals of rational
instruction, but no writers came forward. I confine

myself to recording the fact without going into the causes of it. Two books were afterwards adopted for reading in school. They were not written for school, but they were translated for the Modern School and were very useful. One was called *The Note Book*, the other *Colonisation and Patriotism*. Both were collections of passages from writers of every country on the injustices connected with patriotism, the horrors of war, and the iniquity of conquest. The choice of these works was vindicated by the excellent influence they had on the minds of the children, as we shall see from the little essays of the children which appeared in the *Bulletin*, and the fury with which they were denounced by the reactionary press and politicians.

Many think that there is not much difference between secular and rationalist education, and in various articles and propagandist speeches the two were taken to be synonymous. In order to correct this error I published the following article in the *Bulletin* :—

> The word *education* should not be accompanied by any qualification. It means simply the need and duty of the generation which is in the full development of its powers to prepare the rising generation and admit it to the patrimony of human knowledge. This is an entirely rational ideal, and it will be fully realised in some future age, when men are wholly freed from their prejudices and superstitions.
>
> In our efforts to realise this ideal we find ourselves confronted with religious education and political education : to these we must oppose rational and scientific instruction. The type of religious educa-

tion is that given in the clerical and convent schools of all countries ; it consists of the smallest possible quantity of useful knowledge and a good deal of Christian doctrine and sacred history. Political education is the kind established some time ago in France, after the fall of the Empire, the object of which is to exalt patriotism and represent the actual public administration as the instrument of the common welfare.

Sometimes the qualification *free* or *secular* is applied abusively and maliciously to education, in order to distract or alienate public opinion. Orthodox people, for instance, call *free schools* certain schools which they establish in opposition to the really free tendency of modern pædagogy ; and many are called *secular schools* which are really political, patriotic, and anti-humanitarian.

Rational education is lifted above these illiberal forms. It has, in the first place, no regard to religious education, because science has shown that the story of creation is a myth and the gods legendary ; and therefore religious education takes advantage of the credulity of the parents and the ignorance of the children, maintaining the belief in a supernatural being to whom people may address all kinds of prayers. This ancient belief, still unfortunately widespread, has done a great deal of harm, and will continue to do so as long as it persists. The mission of education is to show the child, by purely scientific methods, that the more knowledge we have of natural products, their qualities, and the way to use them, the more industrial, scientific, and artistic commodities we shall have for the support and comfort of life, and men and women will issue in larger numbers from our schools with a determination to cultivate every branch of knowledge and action, under the guidance of reason and the inspiration of science and art, which will adorn life and reform society.

We will not, therefore, lose our time praying to an imaginary God for things which our own exertions alone can procure.

On the other hand, our teaching has nothing to do with politics. It is our work to form individuals in the full possession of all their faculties, while politics would subject their faculties to other men. While religion has, with its divine power, created a positively abusive power and retarded the development of humanity, political systems also retard it by encouraging men to depend for everything on the will of others, on what are supposed to be men of a superior character—on those, in a word, who, from tradition or choice, exercise the profession of politics. It must be the aim of the rational schools to show the children that there will be tyranny and slavery as long as one man depends upon another, to study the causes of the prevailing ignorance, to learn the origin of all the traditional practices which give life to the existing social system, and to direct the attention of the pupils to these matters.

We will not, therefore, lose our time seeking from others what we can get for ourselves.

In a word, our business is to imprint on the minds of the children the idea that their condition in the social order will improve in proportion to their knowledge and to the strength they are able to develop ; and that the era of general happiness will be the more sure to dawn when they have discarded all religious and other superstitions, which have up to the present done so much harm. On that account there are no rewards or punishments in our schools ; no alms, no

F

medals or badges in imitation of the religious and patriotic schools, which might encourage the children to believe in talismans instead of in the individual and collective power of beings who are conscious of their ability and knowledge.

Rational and scientific knowledge must persuade the men and women of the future that they have to expect nothing from any privileged being (fictitious or real) ; and that they may expect all that is reasonable from themselves and from a freely organised and accepted social order.

I then appealed in the *Bulletin* and the local press to scientific writers who were eager for the progress of the race to supply us with text-books on these lines. They were, I said, "to deliver the minds of the pupils from all the errors of our ancestors, encourage them in the love of truth and beauty, and keep from them the authoritarian dogmas, venerable sophisms, and ridiculous conventionalities which at present disgrace our social life." A special note was added in regard to the teaching of arithmetic :—

The way in which arithmetic has hitherto been generally taught has made it a powerful instrument for impressing the pupils with the false ideals of the capitalist règime which at present presses so heavily on society. The Modern School, therefore, invites essays on the subject of the reform of the teaching of arithmetic, and requests those friends of rational and scientific instruction who are especially occupied with mathematics to draw up a series of easy and practical problems, in which there shall be no reference to wages, economy, and profit. These exercises must deal with agricultural and industrial production, the just distribution of the raw material and the manufactured articles, the means of communication, the transport of merchandise, the comparison of human labour with mechanical, the benefits of machinery, public works, etc.   In a word, the Modern School wants a number of problems showing what arithmetic really ought to be—the science of the social economy (taking the word "economy" in its etymological sense of "good distribution").

The exercises will deal with the four fundamental operations (integrals, decimals, and fractions), the metrical system, proportion, compounds and alloys, the squares and cubes of numbers, and the extraction of square and cube roots.   As those who respond to this appeal are, it is hoped, inspired rather with the ideal of a right education of children than with the desire of profit, and as we wish to avoid the common practice in such circumstances, we shall not appoint judges or offer any prizes.   The Modern School will publish the Arithmetic which best serves its purpose, and will come to an amicable agreement with the author as to his fee.

A later note in the *Bulletin* was addressed to teachers :—

We would call the attention of all who dedicate themselves to the noble ideal of the rational teaching of children and the preparation of the young to take a fitting share in life to the announcements of a *Compendium of Universal History* by Clémence Jacquinet, and *The Adventures of Nono* by Jean Grave, which will be found on the cover.[1]   The

---

[1] It should be stated that both the writers are Anarchists, in the sense I have indicated in the Preface.   Except on special subjects—the famous geographer Odón de Buen, for instance,

works which the Modern School has published or proposes to publish are intended for all free and rational teaching institutions, centres of social study, and parents, who resent the intellectual restrictions which dogma of all kinds—religious, political, and social—imposes in order to maintain privilege at the expense of the ignorant. All who are opposed to Jesuitism and to conventional lies, and to the errors transmitted by tradition and routine, will find in our publications truth based upon evidence. As we have no desire of profit, the price of the works represents almost their intrinsic value or material cost ; if there is any profit from the sale of them, it will be spent upon subsequent publications.

In a later number of the *Bulletin* (No. 6, second year) the distinguished geographer Elisée Reclus wrote, at my request, a lengthy article on the teaching of geography. In a letter which Reclus afterwards wrote me from the Geographical Institute at Brussels, replying to my request that he should recommend a text-book, he said that there was " no text-book for the teaching of geography in elementary schools "; he " did not know one that was not tainted with religious or patriotic poison, or, what is worse, administrative routine." He recommended that the teachers should use no manual in the Modern School, which he cordially commended (February 26, 1903).

co-operated with Ferrer in regard to geography—no other writers were likely to embody Ferrer's ideals. All, however, were as opposed to violence as Ferrer himself, and Mr. W. Archer has shown in his life of Ferrer that the charges brought against Mme. Jacquinet by Ferrer's persecutors at his trial are officially denied by our Egyptian authorities.—J. M.

In the following number (7) of the *Bulletin* I published the following note on the origin of Christianity :—

The older pædagogy, the real, if unavowed, aim of which was to impress children with the uselessness of knowledge, in order that they might be reconciled to their hard conditions and seek consolation in a supposed future life, used reading-books in the elementary school which swarmed with stories, anecdotes, accounts of travels, gems of classical literature, etc. There was a good deal of error mixed with what was sound and useful in this, and the aim was not just. The mystical idea predominated, representing that a relation could be established between a Supreme Being and men by means of priests, and this priesthood was the chief foundation of the existence of both the privileged and the disinherited, and the cause of much of the evil that they endured.

Among other books of this class, all tainted with the same evil, we remember one which inserted an academic discourse, a marvel of Spanish eloquence, in praise of the Bible. The gist of it is expressed in the barbarous declaration of Omar when he condemned the Library of Alexandria to the flames : " The whole truth is contained in the sacred book. If those other books are true, they are superfluous ; if they are not true, they should be burned."

The Modern School, which seeks to form free minds, with a sense of responsibility, fitted to experience a complete development of their powers, which is the one aim of life, must necessarily adopt a very different kind of reading-book, in harmony with its method of teaching. For this reason, as it teaches established truth and is interested in the struggle between light and darkness, it has deemed it necessary to produce a critical work which will enlighten the mind of the child with positive facts. These may not be appreciated in childhood, but will later, in manhood, when the child takes its place in social life and in the struggle against the errors, conventions, hypocrisies, and infamies which conceal themselves under the cloak of mysticism. This work reminds us that our books are not merely intended for children; they are destined also for the use of the Adult Schools which are being founded on every side by associations of workers, Freethinkers, Co-operators, social students, and other progressive bodies who are eager to correct the illiteracy of our nation, and remove that great obstacle to progress.

We believe that the section of Malvert's work (*Science and Religion*) which we have entitled "The Origin of Christianity" will be useful for this purpose. It shows the myths, dogmas, and ceremonies of the Christian religion in their original form; sometimes as exoteric symbols concealing a truth known to the initiated, sometimes as adaptations of earlier beliefs, imposed by sheer routine and preserved by malice. As we are convinced and have ample evidence of the usefulness of our work, we offer it to the public with the hope that it will bear the fruit which we anticipate. We have only to add that certain passages which are unsuitable for children have been omitted; the omissions are indicated, and adults may consult the passages in the complete edition.

Chapter XII.

SUNDAY LECTURES

The Modern School did not confine itself to the instruction of children. Without for a moment sacrificing its predominant character and its chief object, it also undertook the instruction of the people. We arranged a series of public lectures on Sundays, and they were attended by the pupils and other members of their families, and a large number of workers who were anxious to learn.

The earlier lectures were wanting in method and continuity, as we had to employ lecturers who were quite competent in regard to their own subjects, but gave each lecture without regard to what preceded or followed. On other occasions, when we had no lecturer, we substituted useful readings. The general public attended assiduously, and our advertisements in the Liberal press of the district were eagerly scanned.

In view of these results, and in order to encourage the disposition of the general public, I held a consultation with Dr. Andrés Martínez Vargas and Dr. Odón de Buen, Professors at the Barcelona University, on the subject of creating a popular university in the Modern School. In this the science which is given—or, rather, sold—by the State to a privileged few in the universities should be given gratuitously to the general public, by way of restitution, as every human being has a right to know, and science, which is produced by observers and workers of all ages and countries, ought not to be restricted to a class.

From that time the lectures became continuous and regular, having regard to the different branches of knowledge of the two lecturers. Dr. Martínez Vargas expounded physiology and hygiene, and Dr. Odón de Buen geography and natural science, on alternate Sundays, until we began to be persecuted. Their teaching was eagerly welcomed by the pupils of the Modern School, and the large audiences of mixed children and adults. One of the Liberal journals of Barcelona, in giving an account of the work, spoke of the function as "the scientific Mass."

The eternal light - haters, who maintain their privileges on the ignorance of the people, were greatly exasperated to see this centre of enlightenment shining so vigorously, and did not delay long to urge the authorities, who were at their disposal, to extinguish it brutally. For my part, I resolved to put the work on the firmest foundation I could conceive.

I recall with the greatest pleasure that hour we devoted once a week to the confraternity of culture. I inaugurated the lectures on December 15, 1901, when Don Ernesto Vendrell spoke of Hypatia as a martyr to the ideals of science and beauty, the victim of the fanatical Bishop Cyril of Alexandria. Other lectures were given on subsequent Sundays, as I said, until, on October 5, 1902, the lectures were organised in regular courses of science. On that day Dr. Andrés Martínez Vargas, Professor of the Faculty of Medicine (child diseases) at Barcelona University, gave his first lecture. He dealt with the hygiene of the school, and expounded its principles in plain terms adapted to the minds of his hearers. Dr. Odón de Buen, Professor of the Faculty of Science, dealt with the usefulness of the study of natural history.

The press was generally in sympathy with the Modern School, but when the programme of the third scholastic year appeared some of the local journals, the *Noticiero Universal* and the *Diario de Barcelona*, broke out. Here is a passage that deserves recording as an illustration of the way in which conservative journals dealt with progressive subjects :—

> We have seen the prospectus of an educational centre established in this city, which professes to have nothing to do with " dogmas and systems." It proposes to liberate everybody from "authoritarian dogmas, venerable sophisms, and ridiculous conventions." It seems to us that this means that the first thing to do is to tell the boys and girls—it is a mixed school—that there is no God, an admirable way of forming good children, especially young women who are destined to be wives and mothers.

The writer continues in this ironical manner for some time, and ends as follows :—

> This school has the support of a professor of Natural Science (Dr. Odón de Buen) and another of the Faculty of Medicine. We do not name the latter, as there may be some mistake in including

him among the men who lend their support to such a work.

These insidious clerical attacks were answered by the anti-clerical journals of Barcelona at the time.

CHAPTER XIII.

THE RESULTS

AT the beginning of the second scholastic year I once more drew up a programme. Let us, I said, confirm our earlier programme; vindicated by results, approved in theory and practice, the principle which from the first informed our work and governs the Modern School is now unshakable.

Science is the sole mistress of our life. Inspired with this thought, the Modern School proposes to give the children entrusted to it *a mental vitality of their own*, so that when they leave our control they will continue to be the mortal enemies of all kinds of prejudices and will form their own ideas, individually and seriously, on all subjects.

Further, as education does not consist merely in the training of the mind, but must include the emotions and the will, we shall take the utmost care in the training of the child that its intellectual impressions are converted into the sap of sentiment. When this attains a certain degree of intensity, it spreads through the whole being, colouring and refining the individual character. And as the conduct of the youth revolves entirely in the sphere of character, he must learn to adopt science as the sole mistress of his life.

To complete our principle we must state that we are enthusiastically in favour of mixed education, so that, having the same education, the woman may become the real companion of man, and work with him for the regeneration of society. This task has hitherto been confined to man; it is time that the moral influence of woman was enlisted in it. Science will illumine and guide her rich vein of sentiment, and utilise her character for the welfare of the race. Knowing that the chief need in this country is a knowledge of natural science and hygiene, the Modern School intends to help to supply it. In this it has the support of Dr. de Buen and Dr. Vargas, who lecture, alternately, on their respective subjects.

On June 30, 1903, I published in the *Bulletin* the following declaration :—

> We have now passed two years in expounding our principles, justifying them by our practice, and enjoying the esteem of all who have co-operated in our work. We do not see in this any other triumph than that we are able to confirm confidently all that we have proclaimed. We have overcome the obstacles which were put in our way by interest and prejudice, and we intend to persevere in it, counting always on that progressive comradeship which dispels the darkness of ignorance with its strong light. We resume work next September, after the autumn vacation. We are delighted to be able to repeat what we said last year. The Modern School and its *Bulletin* renew their life, for they have filled, with some measure of satisfaction, a deeply-felt need. Without making promises or programmes, we will persevere to the limit of our powers.

In the same number of the *Bulletin* was published the following list of the pupils who had attended the school during the first two years :—

| MONTHS. | GIRLS. | | BOYS. | | TOTAL. | |
	1901–2.	1902–3.	1901–2.	1902–3.	1st Yr.	2nd Yr.
Opening day	12	—	18	—	30	—
September	16	23	23	40	39	63
October	18	28	25	40	43	68
November	21	31	29	40	50	71
December	22	31	30	40	52	71
January	22	31	32	44	54	75
February	23	31	32	48	55	79
March	25	33	34	47	59	80
April	26	32	37	48	63	80
May	30	33	38	48	68	81
June	32	34	38	48	70	82

At the beginning of the third year I published with special pleasure the following article in the *Bulletin* on the progress of the School :—

On the eighth of the present month we opened the new scholastic year. A large number of pupils, their relatives, and members of the general public who were in sympathy with our work and lectures, filled the recently enlarged rooms, and, before the commencement of the function, inspected the collections which give the school the appearance of a museum of science. The function began with a short address from the director, who formally declared the opening of the third year of school life, and said that, as they now had more experience and were encouraged by success, they would carry out energetically the ideal of the Modern School.

Dr. de Buen congratulated us on the enlargement of the School, and supported its aims. Education should, he said, reflect nature, as knowledge can only consist in our perception of what actually exists. On the part of his children, who study at the School and live in the neighbourhood, he paid a tribute to the good-comradeship among the pupils, with whom they played and studied in a perfectly natural way. He said that even in orthodox education, or rather on the part of the professors engaged in it, there were, for all its archaic features, certain tendencies similar to those embodied in the Modern School. This might be gathered from his own presence, and that of Dr. Vargas and other professors. He announced that there was already a similar school at Guadala- jara, or that one would shortly be opened there, built by means of a legacy left for the purpose by a humanitarian. He wished to contribute to the redemption of children and their liberation from ignorance and superstition ; and he expressed a hope and very strong wish that wealthy people would, at their death, restore their goods in this way to the social body, instead of leaving them to secure an imaginary happiness beyond the grave.

Dr. Martínez Vargas maintained, against all who thought otherwise, that the purely scientific and rational education given in the Modern School is the proper basis of instruction ; no better can be conceived for maintaining the relations of the children with their families and society, and it is the only way to form, morally and intellectually, the men of the future. He was glad to hear that the scholastic hygiene which had been practised in the

Modern School during the previous two years, involving a periodical examination of the children, and expounded in the public lectures, had received the solemn sanction of the Hygienic Congress lately held at Brussels.

Going on to resume his lectures, and as a means of enforcing oral instruction by visual perception, he exhibited a series of lantern-slides illustrating various hygienic exercises, certain types of disease, unhealthy organs, etc., which the speaker explained in detail. An accident to the lantern interrupted the pictures ; but the professor continued his explanations, speaking of the mischievous effects of corsets, the danger of microbic infection by trailing dresses or by children playing with soil, insanitary houses and workshops, etc., and promised to continue his medical explanations during the coming year.

The audience expressed its pleasure at the close of the meeting, and the sight of the great joy of the pupils was some consolation amid the hardships of the present, and a good augury for the future.

Chapter XIV.

A DEFENSIVE CHAPTER

Our programme for the third scholastic year (1903-4) was as follows :—

> To promote the progressive evolution of childhood by avoiding all anachronistic practices, which are merely obstacles placed by the past to any real advance towards the future, is, in sum, the predominant aim of the Modern School. Neither dogmas nor systems, moulds which confine vitality to the narrow exigencies of a transitory form of society, will be taught. Only solutions approved by the facts, theories accepted by reason, and truths confirmed by evidence, shall be included in our lessons, so that each mind shall be trained to control a will, and truths shall irradiate the intelligence, and, when applied in practice, benefit the whole of humanity without any unworthy and disgraceful exclusiveness.

> Two years of success are a sufficient guarantee to us. They prove, in the first place, the excellence of mixed education, the brilliant result—the triumph, we would almost say—of an elementary common sense over prejudice and tradition. As we think it advisable, especially that the child may know what is happening about it, that physical and natural science and hygiene should be taught, the Modern School will continue to have the services of Dr. de

Buen and Dr. Vargas. They will lecture on alternate Sundays, from eleven to twelve, on their respective subjects in the school-room. These lectures will complete and further explain the classes in science held during the week.

It remains only to say that, always solicitous for the success of our work of reform, we have enriched our scholastic material by the acquisition of new collections which will at once assist the understanding and give an attractiveness to scientific knowledge ; and that, as our rooms are now not large enough for the pupils, we have acquired other premises in order to have more room and give a favourable reply to the petitions for admission which we have received.

The publication of this programme attracted the attention of the reactionary press, as I said. In order to give them a proof of the logical strength of the position of the Modern School, I inserted the following article in the *Bulletin* :—

Modern pædagogy, relieved of traditions and conventions, must raise itself to the height of the rational conception of man, the actual state of knowledge, and the consequent ideal of mankind. If from any cause whatever a different tendency is given to education, and the master does not do his duty, it would be just to describe him as an impostor ; education must not be a means of dominating men for the advantage of their rulers. Unhappily, this is exactly what happens. Society is organised, not in response to a general need and for the realisation of an ideal, but as an institution with a strong determination to maintain its primitive forms, defending them vigorously against every reform, however reasonable it may be.

G

This element of immobility gives the ancient errors the character of sacred beliefs, invests them with great prestige and a dogmatic authority, and arouses conflicts and disturbances which deprive scientific truths of their due efficacy or keep them in suspense. Instead of being enabled to illumine the minds of all and realise themselves in institutions and customs of general utility, they are unhappily restricted to the sphere of a privileged few. The effect is that, as in the days of the Egyptian theocracy, there is an esoteric doctrine for the cultivated and an exoteric doctrine for the lower classes—the classes destined to labour, defence, and misery.

On this account we set aside the mystic and mythical doctrine, the domination and spread of which only befits the earlier ages of human history, and embrace scientific teaching, according to its evidence. This is at present restricted to the narrow sphere of the intellectuals, or is at the most accepted in secret by certain hypocrites who, so that their position may not be endangered, make a public profession of the contrary. Nothing could make this absurd antagonism clearer than the following parallel, in which we see the contrast between the imaginative dreams of the ignorant believer and the rational simplicity of the scientist :—

THE BIBLE.

The Bible contains the annals of the heavens, the earth, and the human race ; like the Deity himself, it contains all that was, is, and will be. On its first page we read of the beginning of time and of things, and on

ANTHROPISM.

One of the main supports of the reactionary system is what we may call " anthropism." I designate by this term that powerful and world-wide group of erroneous opinions which opposes the human organism its last page the end of time and of things. It begins with *Genesis*, which is an idyll, and ends with *Revelation*, which is a funeral chant. *Genesis* is as beautiful as the fresh breeze which sweeps over the world; as the first dawn of light in the heavens; as the first flower that opens in the meadows; as the first word of love spoken by men; as the first appearance of the sun in the east. *Revelation* is as sad as the last palpitation of nature; as the last ray of the sun; as the last breath of a dying man. And between the funeral chant and the idyll there pass in succession before the eyes of God all generations and all peoples. The tribes and the patriarchs go by; the republics and the magistrates; the monarchies and their kings; the empires and their emperors. Babylon and all its abominations go by; Nineveh and all its pomps; Memphis and its priests; Jerusalem and its prophets and temple; Athens and its arts and heroes; Rome and its diadem of conqueror of the world. Nothing lasts but God; all else passes and dies, like the froth that tips the wave.

to the whole of the rest of nature, and represents it as the preordained end of organic creation, an entity essentially distinct from it, a god-like being. Closer examination of this group of ideas shows it to be made up of three different dogmas, which we may distinguish as the *anthropocentric*, the *anthropomorphic*, and the *anthropolatrous*.

1. The *anthropocentric* dogma culminates in the idea that man is the preordained centre and aim of all terrestrial life—or, in a wider sense, of the whole universe. As this error is extremely conducive to man's interest, and as it is intimately connected with the creation-myth of the three great Mediterranean religions, and with the dogmas of the Mosaic, Christian, and Mohammedan theologies, it still dominates the greater part of the civilised world.

2. The *anthropomorphic* dogma, also, is connected with the creation-myth of the three aforesaid religions and of many others. It likens the creation and control of the world by God to the artificial creation of an able engineer or mechanic, and to the administration of

.   .   .   .

A prodigious book, which mankind began to read three and thirty centuries ago, and of which, if it read all day and night, it would not exhaust the wealth. A prodigious book in which all was calculated before the science of arithmetic was invented ; in which the origin of language is told without any knowledge of philology ; in which the revolutions of the stars are described without any knowledge of astronomy ; in which history is recorded without any documents of history ; in which the laws of nature are unveiled without any knowledge of physics. A prodigious book, that sees everything and knows everything ; that knows the thoughts hidden in the hearts of men and those in the mind of God ; that sees what is happening in the abysses of the sea and in the bowels of the earth ; that records or foretells all the catastrophes of nations, and in which are accumulated all the treasures of mercy, of justice, and of vengeance. A book, in fine, which, when the heavens are folded like a gigantic fan, and the earth a wise ruler. God, as creator, sustainer, and ruler of the world, is thus represented after a purely human fashion in his thought and work. Hence it follows that man in turn is god-like. " God made man to his own image and likeness." The older, naive theology is pure "homotheism," attributing human shape, flesh, and blood to the gods. It is more intelligible than the modern mystic theosophy which adores a personal God as an invisible — p r o p e r l y speaking, gaseous — being, yet makes him think, speak, and act in human fashion ; it offers us the paradoxical picture of a gaseous vertebrate.

3. The *anthropolatric* dogma naturally results from this comparison of the activity of God and man ; it ends in the apotheosis of human nature. A further result is the belief in the personal immortality of the soul, and the dualistic dogma of the twofold nature of man, whose "immortal" soul is conceived as the temporary inhabitant of a mortal frame. Thus these three anthropistic dogmas, variously adapted to the respective professions of the

sinks, and the sun withdraws its light, and the stars are extinguished, will remain with God, because it is his eternal word, echoing for ever in the heights.[1] different religions, came at length to be vested with extraordinary importance, and proved to be the source of the most dangerous errors.[2]

In face of this antagonism, maintained by ignorance and self-interest, positive education, which proposes to teach truths that issue in practical justice, must arrange and systematise the established results of natural research, communicate them to children, and thus prepare the way for a more equitable state of society, in which, as an exact expression of sociology, it must work for the benefit of all as well as of the individual. Moses, or whoever was the author of *Genesis*, and all the dogmatisers, with their six days of creation out of nothing after the Creator has passed an eternity in doing nothing, must give place to Copernicus, who showed the revolution of the planets round the sun ; to Galileo, who proclaimed that the sun, not the earth, is the centre of the planetary universe ; to Columbus and others who, believing the earth to be a sphere, set out in search of other peoples, and gave a practical basis to the doctrine of human brotherhood ; to Linnæus and Cuvier, the founders of natural history ; to Laplace, the inventor of the established cosmogony ; to Darwin, the author of the evolutionary doctrine, which explains the formation of species by natural selection ; and to all who, by means of observation and experiment, have discredited the supposed

[1] Extract from a speech delivered by Donoso Cortés at his admission into the Academy.
[2] Haeckel's *Riddle of the Universe*, Chap. I.

revelation, and tell us the real nature of the universe, the earth, and life.

Against the evils engendered by generations sunk in ignorance and superstition, from which so many are now delivered, only to fall into an anti-social scepticism, the best remedy, without excluding others, is to instruct the rising generation in purely humanist principles and in the positive and rational knowledge provided by science. Women educated thus will be mothers in the true sense of the word, not trans-mitters of traditional superstitions ; they will teach their children integrity of life, the dignity of life, social solidarity, instead of a medley of outworn and sterile dogmas and submission to illegitimate hier-archies. Men thus emancipated from mystery, miracle, and distrust of themselves and their fellows, and convinced that they were born, not to die, as the wretched teaching of the mystics says, but to live, will hasten to bring about such social conditions as will give to life its greatest possible development. In this way, preserving the memory of former genera-tions and other frames of mind as a lesson and a warning, we will once for all close the religious period, and enter definitely into that of reason and nature.

In June, 1904, the *Bulletin* published the following figures in regard to the attendance at school. At that time the publications of the Modern School were in use in thirty-two other schools throughout the country, and its influence was thus felt in Seville and Malaga, Tarragona and Cordova, and other towns, as well as Barcelona and the vicinity. The number of scholars in our schools was also steadily rising, as the following table shows :—

LIST OF THE PUPILS IN THE MODERN SCHOOL
DURING THE FIRST THREE YEARS.

MONTHS.	GIRLS.			BOYS.			TOTALS.		
	1901-2.	1902-3.	1903-4.	1901-2.	1902-3.	1903-4.	1st year.	2nd year.	3rd year.
Opening Day	12	—	—	18	—	—	30	—	—
September	16	23	24	23	40	40	39	63	64
October	18	28	43	25	40	59	43	68	102
November	21	31	44	29	40	59	50	71	103
December	22	31	45	30	40	59	52	71	104
January	22	31	47	32	44	60	54	75	107
February	23	31	47	32	48	61	55	79	108
March	25	33	49	34	47	61	59	80	110
April	26	32	50	37	48	61	63	80	111
May	30	33	51	38	48	62	68	81	113
June	32	34	51	38	48	63	70	82	114

CHAPTER XV.

THE INGENUOUSNESS OF THE CHILD

IN the *Bulletin* of September 30, 1903, we published
the work of the pupils in the various classes of the
Modern School, which had been read on the closing
day of the second scholastic year. In these writings,
in which the children are requested to apply their dawn-
ing judgment to some particular subject, the influence
of mind over the inexpert, ingenuous reasoning power,
inspired by the sentiment of justice, is more apparent
than the observance of rules. The judgments are not
perfect from the logical point of view, only because the
child has not the knowledge necessary for the formation of a perfectly sound opinion. This is the opposite of what we usually find, as opinions are generally
founded only on prejudice arising from traditions,
interests, and dogmas.

A boy of twelve, for instance, gave the following
principle for judging the value of nations :—

> To be called civilised, a nation or State must be free
> from the following—

Let me interrupt for a moment to point out that the
young author identifies "civilised" with "just," and
especially that, putting aside prejudice, he describes
certain evils as curable, and regards the healing of

them as an essential condition of justice.   These evils
are :—

    1°. The co-existence of poor and rich, and the re-
sultant exploitation.

    2°. Militarism, a means of destruction employed by
one nation against another, due to the bad organisation of society.

    3°. Inequality, which allows some to rule and com-
mand, and obliges others to humble themselves and
obey.

This principle is fundamental and simple, as we
should expect to find in an imperfectly informed mind,
and it would not enable one to solve a complete socio-
logical problem ; but it has the advantage of keeping
the mind open to fresh knowledge.   It is as if one
asked : What does a sick man need to recover health ?
And the reply is : His suffering must disappear.   This
is a naive and natural reply, and would certainly not
be given by a child brought up in the ordinary way ;
such a child would be taught first to consider the will
of supposed supernatural beings.   It is clear that this
simple way of putting the problem of life does not
shut out the hope of a reasonable solution ; indeed,
the one logically demands the other, as the same
child's essay shows :—

> I do not mean that, if there were no rich, or soldiers,
> or rulers, or wages, people would abuse their liberty
> and welfare, but that, with everybody enjoying a high
> degree of civilisation, there would be universal cor-
> diality and friendship, and science would make much
> greater progress, not being interrupted by wars and
> political stagnation.

A girl of nine made the following sensible observation, which we leave in her own incorrect language :—

> A criminal is condemned to death ; if the murderer deserves this punishment, the man who condemns him and the man who kills him are also murderers ; logically, they ought to die as well, and so humanity would come to an end. It would be better, instead of punishing a criminal by committing another crime, to give him good advice, so that he will not do it again. Besides, if we are all equal, there would be no thieves, or assassins, or rich people, or poor, but all would be equal and love work and liberty.

The simplicity, clearness, and soundness of this observation need no commentary. One can understand our astonishment to hear it from the lips of a tender and very pretty little girl, who looked more like a symbolical representation of truth and justice than a living reality.

A boy of twelve deals with sincerity, and says :—

> The man who is not sincere does not live peacefully ; he is always afraid of being discovered : when one is sincere, if one has done wrong, the sincere declaration relieves the conscience. If a man begins to tell lies in childhood, he will tell bigger lies when he grows up, and may do much harm. There are cases in which one need not be sincere. For instance, if a man comes to our house, flying from the police, and we are asked afterwards if we have seen him, we must deny it ; the contrary would be treachery and cowardice.

It is sad that the mind of a child who regards truth as an incomparable good, "without which it is impossible to live," is induced by certain grave abuses to consider lying a virtue in some cases.

A girl of thirteen writes of fanaticism, and, regarding it as a characteristic of backward countries, she goes on to seek the cause :—

> Fanaticism is the outcome of the state of ignorance and backwardness of women ; on that account Catholics do not want to see women educated, as they are the chief support of their system.

A profound observation on the causes of fanaticism, and the cause of the causes.   Another girl of thirteen indicates the best remedy of the evil in the following lines :—

> The mixed school, for both sexes, is supremely necessary.   The boy who studies, works, and plays in the society of girls learns gradually to respect and help her, and the girl reciprocally ; whereas, if they are educated separately, and the boy is told that the girl is not a good companion and she is worse than he, the boy will not respect women when he is a man, and will regard her as a subject or a slave, and that is the position in which we find women.   So we must all work for the foundation of mixed schools, wherever it is possible, and where it is not possible we must try to remove the difficulties.

A boy of twelve regards the school as worthy of all respect, because we learn in it to read, write, and think, and it is the basis of morality and science; he adds:—

> If it were not for the school we should live like savages, walk naked, eat herbs and raw flesh, and dwell in caves and trees ; that is to say, we should live a brutal life.   In time, as a result of the school,

everybody will be more intelligent, and there will be no wars or inflamed populations, and people will look back on war with horror as a work of death and destruction. It is a great disgrace that there are children who wander in the streets and do not go to school, and when they become men it is more disgraceful. So let us be grateful to our teachers for the patience they show in instructing us, and let us regard the school with respect.

If that child preserves and develops the faculties it exhibits, it will know how to harmonise egoism and altruism for its own good and that of society. A girl of eleven deplores that nations destroy each other in war, and laments the difference of social classes and that the rich live on the work and privation of the poor. She ends :—

Why do not men, instead of killing each other in wars and hating each other for class-differences, devote themselves cheerfully to work and the discovery of things for the good of mankind? Men ought to unite to love each other and live fraternally.[1]

A child of ten, in an essay which is so good that I would insert it whole if space permitted, and if it were not for the identity in sentiment with the previous passages, says of the school and the pupil :—

Reunited under one roof, eager to learn what we

[1] I omit some of Ferrer's short comments on these specimens of reasoning and sentiment, as he regards them. One can recognise the echo of the teacher's words. The children were repeating their catechism. But (1) this is no catechism of violence and class-hatred, and (2) there is a distinct appreciation of the ideas and sentiments on the part of the children. I translate the passages as literally as possible.—J. M.

do not know, without distinction of classes [there
were children of university professors among them,
it will be remembered], we are children of one family
guided to the same end......The ignorant man is a
nullity ; little or nothing can be expected of him.
He is a warning to us not to waste time ; on the
contrary, let us profit by it, and in due course we will
be rewarded. Let us not miss the fruits of a good
school, and, honouring our teachers, our family, and
society, we shall live happily.

A child of ten philosophises on the faults of mankind, which, in her opinion, can be avoided by
instruction and goodwill :—

Among the faults of mankind are lying, hypocrisy,
and egoism. If men, and especially women, were
better instructed, and women were entirely equal
to men, these faults would disappear. Parents would
not send their children to religious schools, which
inculcate false ideas, but to rational schools, where
there is no teaching of the supernatural, which does
not exist ; nor to make war ; but to live in solidarity
and work in common.

We will close with the following essay, written by a
young lady of sixteen, which is correct enough in form
and substance to quote in entirety :—

What inequality there is in the present social
order ! Some working from morning to night without more profit than enough to buy their insufficient
food ; others receiving the products of the workers in
order to enjoy themselves with the superfluous. Why
is this so? Are we not all equal? Undoubtedly we
are ; but society does not recognise it, while some
are destined to work and suffering, and others to

idleness and enjoyment. If a worker shows that he realises the exploitation to which he is subject, he is blamed and cruelly punished, while others suffer the inequality with patience. The worker must educate himself ; and in order to do this it is necessary to found free schools, maintained by the wages which the rich give. In this way the worker will advance more and more, until he is regarded as he deserves, since the most useful mission of society depends on him.

Whatever be the logical value of these ideas, this collection shows the chief aim of the Modern School —namely, that the mind of the child, influenced by what it sees and informed by the positive knowledge it acquires, shall work freely, without prejudice or submission to any kind of sect, with perfect autonomy and no other guide but reason, equal in all, and sanctioned by the cogency of evidence, before which the darkness of sophistry and dogmatic imposition is dispelled.

In December, 1903, the Congress of Railway Workers, which was then held at Barcelona, informed us that, as a part of its programme, the delegates would visit the Modern School. The pupils were delighted, and we invited them to write essays to be read on the occasion of the visit. The visit was prevented by unforeseen circumstances ; but we published in the *Bulletin* the children's essays, which exhaled a delicate perfume of sincerity and unbiassed judgment, graced by the naive ingenuousness of the writers. No suggestion was made to them, and they did not compare notes, yet there was a remarkable agreement in their sentiments.   At another time the pupils of the Workers' School at Badalona sent a greeting to our pupils, and they again wrote essays, from which we compiled a return letter of greeting.[1]

[1] This letter and the preceding essays are given in the Spanish edition.   As they are a repetition of the sentiments expressed in the extracts already given, it is unnecessary to reproduce them here.   Except that I have omitted papers incorporated by Ferrer, but not written by him, this is the only modification I have allowed myself.—J. M.

Chapter XVI.

THE *BULLETIN*

THE Modern School needed and found its organ in the Press. The political and ordinary press, which at one time favoured us and at another time denounced us as dangerous, cannot maintain an impartial attitude. It either gives exaggerated or unmerited praise, or calumnious censures. The only remedy for this was the sincerity and clearness of our own indications. To allow these libels to pass without correction would have done us considerable harm, and the *Bulletin* enabled us to meet them.

The directors published in it the programme of the school, interesting notes about it, statistical details, original pædagogical articles by the teachers, accounts of the progress of rational education in our own and other countries, translations of important articles from foreign reviews and periodicals which were in harmony with the main character of our work, reports of the Sunday lectures, and announcements of the public competitions for the engagement of teachers and of our library.

One of the most successful sections of the *Bulletin* was that devoted to the publication of the ideas of the pupils. Besides showing their individual ideas it revealed the spontaneous manifestation of common sense. Girls and boys, with no appreciable difference in intellect according to sex, in contact with the realities of life as indicated by the teachers, expressed themselves in simple essays which, though sometimes immature in judgment, more often showed the clear logic with which they conceived philosophical, political, or social questions of some importance. The journal was at first distributed without charge among the pupils, and was exchanged with other periodicals; but there was soon a demand for it, and a public subscription had to be opened. When this was done, the *Bulletin* became a philosophical review, as well as organ of the Modern School; and it retained this character until the persecution began and the school was closed. An instance of the important mission of the *Bulletin* will be found in the following article, which I wrote in No. 5 of the fourth year, in order to correct certain secular teachers who had gone astray :—

A certain Workers' School has introduced the novelty of establishing a savings-bank, administered by the pupils. This piece of information, reproduced in terms of great praise by the press as a thing to be imitated, induces us to express our opinion on the subject. While others have their own right to decide and act, we have the same right to criticise, and thus to create a rational public opinion.

In the first place we would observe that the word *economy* is very different from, if not the opposite of, the idea of *saving*. One may teach children the knowledge and practice of economy without necessarily

H

teaching them to save. *Economy* means a prudent and methodical use of one's goods : *saving* means a restriction of one's use of one's goods. By economising, we avoid waste ; by saving, the man who has nothing superfluous deprives himself of what is necessary.

Have the children who are taught to save any superfluous property ? The very name of the society in question assures us that they have not. The workers who send their children to this school live on their wages, the minimum sum, determined by the laws of supply and demand, which is paid for their work by the employers ; and as this wage gives them nothing superfluous, and the social wealth is monopolised by the privileged classes, the workers are far from obtaining enough to live a life in harmony with the progress of civilisation. Hence, when these children of workers, and future workers themselves, are taught to save—which is a voluntary privation under the appearance of interest—they are taught to prepare themselves to submit to privilege. While the intention is to initiate them to the practice of economy, what is really done is to convert them into victims and accomplices of the present unjust order.

The working-class child is a human child, and, as such, it has a right to the development of all its faculties, the satisfaction of all its needs, moral and physical. For that purpose society was instituted. It is not its function to repress or subject the individual, as is selfishly pretended by the privileged and reactionary class, and all who enjoy what others produce ; it has to hold the balance justly between the rights and duties of all members of the commonwealth.

As it is, the individual is asked to sacrifice his

rights, needs, and pleasures to society ; and, as this
disorder demands patience, suffering, and sophistical
reasoning, let us commend economy and blame
saving. We do not think it right to teach children
to look forward to being workers in a social order in
which the average mortality of the poor, who live
without freedom, instruction, or joy, reaches an
appalling figure in comparison with that of the class
which lives in triumph on their labour. Those who,
from sociolatry, would derogate in the least from the
rights of man, should read the fine and vigorous
words of Pi y Margall : "Who art thou to prevent
my use of my human rights? Perfidious and tyran-
nical society, thou wert created to defend, not to
coerce us. Go back to the abyss whence thou
came."

Starting from these principles, and applying them to
pædagogy, we think it necessary to teach children
that to waste any class of objects is contrary to the
general welfare ; that if a child spoils paper, loses
pens, or destroys books, it does an injustice to its
parents and the school. Assuredly one may impress
on the child the need of prudence in order to avoid
getting imperfect things, and remind it of lack of
employment, illness, or age ; but it is not right to
insist that a provision be made out of a salary
which does not suffice to meet the needs of life. That
is bad arithmetic.

The workers have no university training ; they do
not go to the theatre or to concerts ; they never go
into ecstasies before the marvels of art, industry, or
nature ; they have no holiday in which to fill their
lungs with life-giving oxygen ; they are never uplifted
by reading books or reviews. On the contrary, they
suffer all kinds of privations, and may have to endure

crises due to excessive production. It is not the place of teachers to hide these sad truths from the children, and to tell them that a smaller quantity is equal to, if not better than, a larger. In order that the power of science and industry be shared by all, and all be invited to partake of the banquet of life, we must not teach in the school, in the interest of privilege, that the poor should organise the advantages of crumbs and leavings. We must not prostitute education.

On another occasion I had to censure a different departure from our principles :—

We were distressed and indignant on reading the list of contributions voted by the Council of Barcelona for certain popular societies which are interested in education. We read of sums offered to Republican Fraternities and similar societies ; and we find that, instead of rejecting them, they forwarded votes of thanks to the Council.

The meaning of these things in a Catholic and ultra-conservative nation is clear. The Church and the capitalist system only maintain their ascendency by a judicious system of charity and protection. With this they gratify the disinherited class, and continue to enjoy its respect. But we cannot see republicans acting as if they were humble Christians without raising a cry of alarm.

Beware, we repeat, beware ! You are educating your children badly, and taking the wrong path towards reform, in accepting alms. You will neither emancipate yourselves nor your children if you trust in the strength of others, and rely on official or private support. Let the Catholics, ignorant of the realities of life, expect everything of God, or St. Joseph, or some similar being, and, as they have no security that their prayers will be heard in this life, trust to receive a reward after death. Let gamblers in the lottery fail to see that they are morally and materially victimised by their rulers, and trust to receive by chance what they do not earn by energy. But it is sad to see men hold out the hand of a beggar who are united in a revolutionary protest against the present system ; to see them admitting and giving thanks for humiliating gifts, instead of trusting their own energy, intellect, and ability.

Beware, then, all men of good faith ! That is not the way to set up a true education of children, but the way to enslave them.

Chapter XVII.

THE CLOSING OF THE MODERN SCHOOL

I HAVE reached the culmination of my life and my work. My enemies, who are all the reactionaries in the world, represented by the reactionaries of Barcelona and of Spain, believed that they had triumphed by involving me in a charge of attempted assassination. But their triumph proved to be only an episode in the struggle of practical Rationalism against reaction. The shameful audacity with which they claimed sentence of death against me (a claim that was refused on account of my transparent innocence rather than on account of the justice of the court) drew on me the sympathy of all liberal men—all true progressives — in all parts of the world, and fixed attention on the meaning and ideal of the Rational School. There was a universal and uninterrupted movement of protest and admiration for a whole year —from May, 1906, to May and June, 1907—echoed in the Press of every civilised country, and in meetings and other popular manifestations.

It proved in the end that the mortal enemies of our work were its most effective supporters, as they led to the establishment of international Rationalism.

I felt my own littleness in face of this mighty

manifestation. Led always by the light of the ideal, I conceived and carried out the International League for the Rational Education of Children, in the various branches of which, scattered over the world, are found men in the front ranks of culture [Anatole France, Ernst Haeckel, etc.]. It has three organs, *L'École Renovée* in France, the *Bulletin* in Barcelona, and *La Scuola Laica* at Rome, which expound, discuss, and spread all the latest efforts of pædagogy to purify science from all defilement of error, to dispel all credulity, to bring about a perfect harmony between belief and knowledge, and to destroy that privileged esoteric system which has always left an exoteric doctrine to the masses.

This great concentration of knowledge and research must lead to a vigorous action which will give to the future revolution the character of practical manifestation of applied sociology, without passion or demand of revenge, with no terrible tragedies or heroic sacrifices, no sterile movements, no disillusion of zealots, no treacherous returns to reaction. For scientific and rational education will have pervaded the masses, making each man and woman a self-conscious, active, and responsible being, guiding his will according to his judgment, free for ever from the passions inspired by those who exploit respect for tradition and for the charlatanry of the modern framers of political programmes.

If progress thus loses this dramatic character of revolution, it will gain in firmness, stability, and continuity, as evolution. The vision of a rational society, which revolutionaries foresaw in all ages, and which sociologists confidently promise, will rise before the eyes of our successors, not as the mirage of dreamy utopians, but as the positive and merited triumph won by the revolutionary power of reason and science.

The new repute of the educational work of the Modern School attracted the attention of all who appreciated the value of sound instruction. There was a general demand for knowledge of the system. There were numbers of private secular schools, or similar institutions supported by societies, and their directors made inquiry concerning the difference of our methods from theirs. There were constant requests to visit the school and consult me. I gladly satisfied them, removed their doubts, and pressed them to enter on the new way; and at once efforts were made to reform the existing schools, and to create others on the model of the Modern School.

There was great enthusiasm and the promise of mighty things; but one serious difficulty stood in the way : we were short of teachers, and had no means of creating them. Professional teachers had two disadvantages—traditional habits and dread of the contingencies of the future. There were very few who, in an unselfish love of the ideal, would devote themselves to the progressive cause. Instructed young men and women might be found to fill the gap; but how were we to train them? Where could they pass their apprenticeship? Now and again I heard from workers' or political societies that they had decided to open a school ; they would find rooms and appliances, and we could count upon their using our school manuals.   But whenever I asked if they had teachers, they replied in the negative, and thought it would be easy to supply the want.   I had to give in.

Circumstances had made me the director of rationalist education, and I had constant consultations and demands on the part of aspirants for the position of teacher.   This made me realise the defect, and I endeavoured to meet it by private advice and by admitting young assistants in the Modern School. The result was naturally mixed.   There are now worthy teachers who will carry on the work of rational education elsewhere ; others failed from moral or intellectual incapacity.

Not feeling that the pupils of the Modern School who devoted themselves to teaching would find time for their work, I established a Normal School, of which I have already spoken.   I was convinced that, if the key of the social problem is in the scientific and rational school, it is essential, to make a proper use of the key, that fitting teachers be trained for so great a destiny.

As the practical and positive result of my work, I may say that the Modern School of Barcelona was a most successful experiment, and that it was distinguished for two characters :—

1°. While open to successive improvements, it set up a standard of what education should be in a reformed state of society.

2°. It gave an impulse to the spread of this kind of education.

There was up to that time no education in the true sense of the word. There were, for the privileged few in the universities, traditional errors and prejudices, authoritarian dogmas, mixed up with the truths which modern research has brought to light. For the people there was primary instruction, which was, and is, a method of taming children. The school was a sort of riding-school, where natural energies were subdued in order that the poor might suffer their hard lot in silence. Real education, separated from faith—education that illumines the mind with the light of evidence—is the creation of the Modern School.

During its ephemeral existence[1] it did a marvellous amount of good. The child admitted to the school and kept in contact with its companions rapidly changed its habits, as I have observed. It cultivated cleanliness, avoided quarrels, ceased to be cruel to animals, took no notice in its games of the barbarous spectacle which we call the national entertainment [bull-fight], and, as its mind was uplifted and its sentiments purified, it deplored the social injustices which abound on the very face of life. It detested war, and would not admit that national glory, instead of consisting in the highest possible moral development and happiness of a people, should be placed in conquest and violence.

[1] The Modern School was closed after Ferrer's arrest in 1906. —J. M.

The influence of the Modern School, extended to other schools which had been founded on its model and were maintained by various working-men societies, penetrated the families by means of the children. Once they were touched by the influence of reason and science they were unconsciously converted into teachers of their own parents, and these in turn diffused the better standards among their friends and relatives.

This spread of our influence drew on us the hatred of Jesuitism of all kinds and in all places, and this hatred inspired the design which ended in the closing of the Modern School. It is closed ; but in reality it is concentrating its forces, defining and improving its plan, and gathering the strength for a fresh attempt to promote the true cause of progress.

That is the story of what the Modern School was, is, and ought to be.

EPILOGUE

By J. M.

"THAT is the story of what the Modern School was, is, and ought to be." When Ferrer wrote this, in the summer of 1908, he was full of plans for the continuation of his work in various ways. He was fostering such free schools as the Government still permitted. He was promoting his "popular university," and multiplying works of science and sociology for the million. His influence was growing, and he saw with glad eyes the light breaking on the ignorant masses of his fellows. In the summer of 1909 he came to England to study the system of moral instruction which, under the inspiration of the Moral Instruction League, is used in thousands of English schools. A friend in London begged him never to return to Spain, as his life was sought. He knew it, but nothing would divert him from his ideal. And three months later he was shot, among the graves of criminals, in the trenches of Montjuich.

Form your own opinion of him from his words. He conceals nothing. He was a rebel against religious traditions and social inequalities; he wished children to become as resentful of poverty and superstition as he. There is no law of Spain, or of any other country, that forbids such enterprise as his. He might be shot in Russia, of course; for the law has been suspended there for more than a decade. In Spain men had to lie in order to take his life.

With the particular value of his scheme of education I am not concerned. He was well acquainted with pædagogical literature, and there were few elementary schools in Spain to equal his. Writers who have spoken slightingly of his school, apart from its social dogmas, know little or nothing about it. Ferrer was in close and constant association with two of the ablest professors in the university of Barcelona, one of whom sent his children to the school, and with distinguished scholars in other lands. There was more stimulating work done in the Modern School than, probably, in any other elementary school in Spain, if not elsewhere. All that can be questioned is the teaching of an explicit social creed to the children. Ferrer would have rejoined that there was not a school in Europe that does not teach an explicit social creed. But, however we may differ from his creed, we cannot fail to recognise the elevated and unselfish idealism of the man, and deplore the brutality and illegality with which his genial life was prematurely brought to a close.

THE ATHEIST VIEWPOINT

AN ARNO PRESS / NEW YORK TIMES COLLECTION

Amberley, [John Russell], Viscount. **An Analysis of Religious Belief.** 1877.

Atheist Magazines: A Sampling, 1927–1970. New Introduction by Madalyn Murray O'Hair. 1972.

Besant, Annie. **The Freethinker's Text-Book:** Part II—Christianity. n.d.

[Burr, William Henry.] **Revelations of Antichrist.** 1879.

Cardiff, Ira D. **What Great Men Think of Religion.** 1945.

Champion of Liberty: Charles Bradlaugh. 1934.

Cohen, Chapman. **Primitive Survivals in Modern Thought.** 1935.

Drews, Arthur. **The Witnesses to the Historicity of Jesus.** Translated by Joseph McCabe. 1912.

Ferrer [y Guardia], Francisco. **The Origins and Ideals of the Modern School.** Translated by Joseph McCabe. 1913.

Foote, G. W. and W. P. Ball, editors. **The Bible Handbook.** 1961.

Gibbon, Edward. **History of Christianity.** 1883.

Holyoake, George Jacob. **The History of the Last Trial by Jury for Atheism in England.** 1851.

Komroff, Manuel, editor. **The Apocrypha or Non-Canonical Books of the Bible:** The King James Version. 1936.

Lewis, Joseph. **Atheism and Other Addresses.** 1960.

McCarthy, William. **Bible, Church and God.** 1946.

Macdonald, George E. **Fifty Years of Freethought.** 1929, 1931. Two volumes in one.

Manhattan, Avro. **Catholic Imperialism and World Freedom.** 1952.

Meslier, Jean. **Superstition in All Ages.** Translated from the French original by Anna Knoop. 1890.

Nietzsche, Friedrich. **The Antichrist.** 1930.

O'Hair, Madalyn Murray. **What on Earth Is an Atheist!** 1969.

Robertson, J. M. **A Short History of Freethought.** 1957.

Russell, Bertrand. **Atheism: Collected Essays, 1943–1949.** 1972.

Shelley, Percy Bysshe. **Selected Essays on Atheism.** (n.d.) 1972.

Teller, Woolsey. **The Atheism of Astronomy.** 1938.

Wells, H. G. **Crux Ansata:** An Indictment of the Roman Catholic Church. 1944.